Valperga

Volume 2

Or, The life and adventures of Castruccio, prince of Lucca

Mary Wollstonecraft Shelley

Alpha Editions

This edition published in 2024

ISBN : 9789362920171

Design and Setting By
Alpha Editions
www.alphaedis.com
Email - info@alphaedis.com

As per information held with us this book is in Public Domain.
This book is a reproduction of an important historical work. Alpha Editions uses the best technology to reproduce historical work in the same manner it was first published to preserve its original nature. Any marks or number seen are left intentionally to preserve its true form.

Contents

CHAPTER I .... - 1 -
CHAPTER II .... - 10 -
CHAPTER III .... - 22 -
CHAPTER IV .... - 30 -
CHAPTER V .... - 40 -
CHAPTER VI .... - 48 -
CHAPTER VII .... - 57 -
CHAPTER VIII .... - 69 -
CHAPTER IX .... - 77 -
CHAPTER X .... - 88 -
CHAPTER XI .... - 98 -
CHAPTER XII .... - 105 -

CHAPTER I

Conference of Castruccio and Galeazzo Visconti—of Castruccio and the Bishop of Ferrara.

When Castruccio and Euthanasia arrived at Florence, they found the citizens celebrating a festival: the bells were ringing; the country people were flocking into the town; and the youths of both sexes, of the highest rank, and richly dressed, were parading the streets, covered with wreaths of flowers, and singing the poems of Dante, or his friend Guido, to the accompaniment of many instruments. Castruccio said: "I must ask you, fair Euthanasia, who are so learned in Florentine customs, to inform me of the meaning of this gaiety."

"Indeed, I am entirely ignorant. I know that during peace joyful meetings take place every May, among the young nobility; but this seems a general festivity. Let us ask that grave gentleman in the black capuchin, if he knows the reason of a merriment, which at least has not communicated itself to his face."

The man, on being asked, replied: "You must be but lately arrived, not to have heard of the cause of our rejoicings; the Florentines, Madonna, are celebrating the occurrence of a most favourable omen with which God and St. John have blest our city. Yesterday one of the lionesses kept at the expence of the republic, brought forth five whelps."

"And is this the momentous occasion of so much serious amusement?" asked Castruccio, laughing.

"My lord," said the man, "you are a stranger in this town; or you would not find cause for laughter in this event. The Florentines keep a number of lions, as the signs and symbols of their strength; and God and St. John have plainly manifested on many occasions, that the prosperity of Florence, and the welfare of the lions are bound together. Three of the finest and largest died on the eve of the fatal battle of Monte Catini."

"So these wise republicans, whom you, dear Euthanasia, so much vaunt, believe in these childish omens. I would wager my best charger, that their records are full of the influence of stars, and the appearance of comets!"

"And I do not at all know that you would lose: indeed their noblest citizens have a great faith in astrology and portents. If you speak of a scarcity, they will tell of a meteor; if you say that the king of France has lost a battle, they will assure you that the whole kingdom has become, by the will of God and St. John, weaker and more miserable, ever since Philippe le Bel seized upon the Florentine usurers. We love to find a cause for every event, believing that, if we can fit but one link to another, we are on the high road for discovering the last secrets of nature. You smile at the celebration of the birth of these lion's whelps; yet I own that it pleases me; how innocent, yet how active, must the imagination of that people be, who can find cause for universal joy in such an event!

"It is this same imagination more usefully and capaciously employed, that makes them decree the building of the most extensive and beautiful building of modern times. The men who have conceived the idea, and contributed their money towards the erection of the Duomo, will never see its completion; but their posterity will, and, if they be not degenerate, will glory in the noble spirit of their ancestors. Many years ago, when the Florentines warred with the Siennese, they took by storm a tower of great strength, which commanded a most important pass. They destroyed the tower; and, when half demolished, they filled it up with earth, and planted there an olive tree, which still flourishes, an emblem of the peace which would follow their conquests."

Castruccio staid only a few days at Florence; and, recommending himself to the constancy and love of Euthanasia, he took an affectionate leave of her, and hastened on his journey to Rovigo, where he had promised to join Galeazzo Visconti.

Galeazzo, having now succeeded to his father in the tyranny of Milan, was the most powerful chief of Lombardy. He was about thirty-five years of age: he had all the characteristics of an Italian face, arched brows, black eyes, an aquiline nose, and a figure where there was some strength and little grace. He had a great portion of talent, quickness in the combination of plans, yet not sufficient patience to watch their progress, or perseverance to carry them through. He was crafty, ambitious, and vain; yet, where his own interests were not concerned, he was good-natured, and on all occasions exceeded even the Italians in the courtesy of his demeanour. He had seen much of the world, and suffered many misfortunes; this gave him a pliancy of disposition, as well as of manner, which made him appear more kind-hearted than he really was; for in truth he never for a moment lost sight of his own interest; and, if he sometimes wandered from the path which led to its attainment, want of judgement, and not of inclination, caused the error.

He wished to attach Castruccio to his party and designs. He saw in him the head of the Ghibeline faction in Tuscany, and the tamer of his Florentine enemies. He felt that his own situation was precarious; but, if he could gain Castruccio for his ally, he hoped to awe his enemies. More than all, he desired the destruction of the Guelph strong-hold, Florence; and Castruccio was to become its destroyer. He heard of his peace with that city with dismay; he trusted it could not last; but the very name of it blasted his hopes. He wished to see the consul, and to win him to the plan which he had conceived would conduct to the full ascendancy of the Ghibelines; and, circumstances leading him to Rovigo, he had intreated Castruccio to visit him there, making the intended restoration of Ferrara to the marquess of Este the pretence of this request.

The friends met with every demonstration of regard. Galeazzo watched with care every word, by which Castruccio might reveal his intentions, before he would venture to communicate his own wishes. Their first topic of conversation was the immediate business before them, the restoration of the marquess Obizzo to the sovereignty of Ferrara. "This town," said Galeazzo, "which so long obeyed the Este family, is now in the hands of the Guelphs, and the vicar of the Pope, with a couple of hundred Gascon soldiers for a garrison, keeps possession of it. The people, fleeced by the excellent policy of the Roman court, whose first, second, and third maxim is to fill its own coffers, eagerly desire the restoration of their rightful prince. We have often thought of besieging the town; but that would be a long and expensive business, and even its success would be doubtful; for, if the Ghibelines raised their war-cry, all the Guelph foxes would unearth themselves and have at them, and you know that our lands are much overstocked by this vermin. Stratagem is a surer and a far easier mode of warfare, and not half so bloody as the regular way; we have so many friends within the walls, that I doubt not we should succeed, if a proper communication were established between us. The bishop, who, though a churchman, is our sure friend, sent us a message some days ago, which, although mystically worded, seemed to say that he would betray the town into our hands, if we would commission one of our chiefs to treat with him; for he refused to disclose his project to an underling. Now, you, my good friend, must undertake this task; we are all of us too well known to get admission into the city; but a slight disguise will take you safely past their guards, and I doubt neither of the bishop Marsilio's power or inclination."

Castruccio acceded to his friend's request; and in the evening he was introduced to the marquess of Este, who received him with deference and distinction.

The next morning, when he and Galeazzo rode out together, Galeazzo said: "I am sure, my dear Castruccio, I can never shew myself sufficiently grateful for your kindness in quitting Lucca at my request, and wandering away from your government, which I ardently hope will not suffer from your absence. But I feel less remorse, since the truce you have concluded with Florence must afford you some leisure."

"Not a truce, but a better thing; I have concluded a peace."

appearance. Castruccio, who by his intercourse with the world had learned always to honour age, approached him with respect, and disclosed to him his rank and mission. The bishop replied:

"My noble lord, the marquess has done that which I have long desired, in sending to me one to whom I may intrust the important secret, which I do not doubt will be the means of his re-establishment in his government. This evening my friends will assemble at my palace; with their counsel all shall be arranged, the means disclosed to you by which I propose to deliver Ferrara into the hands of its rightful prince, and the day fixed for the commencement of the enterprize."

The bishop and Castruccio continued together the whole day, both mutually delighted with each other; and, as is often the case where sympathy of opinion and feeling exists, they became as intimate in a few hours, as in other circumstances an intercourse of years would have effected. Castruccio had a great taste for theological knowledge, and the bishop, as a man of the world, was delighted with the conversation and remarks of one who had passed through so many scenes, and visited so many nations. Confidence quickly arose between them; so well did each seem to understand the feelings and character of the other. The bishop was a Ghibeline; but his motives were pure: his indignation at the corruptions of the Papal court, and his disapprobation of the faction and brawls which appeared to him inseparable from a republic, attached him strongly to the Imperial party, and to those lords who, reigning peacefully over a people who loved them, seemed to him to ensure the quiet of Italy.

In the evening the partizans of the marquess of Este assembled at the episcopal palace to deliberate on their projects. Castruccio was introduced among them, and received with cordiality and respect by all. The assembly consisted of nearly the whole nobility of Ferrara, chiefly indeed Ghibelines, but there were even some Guelphs, disgusted by the introduction of foreign troops, and the haughtiness and tyranny of their governors. The government however was formidable; they possessed the gates, and the fortress; their armed guard was numerous and faithful; and the restoration of Obizzo could be achieved by stratagem alone.

In one corner of the vast apartment in which the assembly sat, were two women. One was old, and dressed in the fashion of an age gone by: she was in black as a widow; her vest was close and strait, trimmed with beads, and made of black cloth; a black veil covered her head, and her capuchin thrown aside discovered the years and wrinkles of the venerable wearer. It was impossible to judge of the age, and hardly of the sex, of the figure that sat beside her; for her capuchin was wrapped closely round her form, and the hood drawn over her face, as she sat silently, turned away from the company, in the darkest part of the room.

The bishop at length addressed Castruccio: "My lord," said he, "you now possess the details of our plan, and may perceive the sincerity of our intention, and the eagerness of our desire to receive again our rightful prince: it alone remains to shew you the secret entrance of which I spoke, and to fix the day for our attempt."

The old lady, who had been hitherto silent, now turned quickly round, and said: "My brother, Beatrice ought to name the fortunate day on which we may undertake this work. Speak, my child, and may the holy Virgin inspire your words!"

As she spoke, she threw back the hood of her young companion; and Castruccio gazed on her exquisite and almost divine beauty. Her deep black eyes, half concealed by their heavy lids, her curved lips, and face formed in a perfect oval, the rising colour that glowed in her cheeks which, though her complexion was pure and delicate, were tinged by the suns of Italy, formed a picture such as Guido has since imagined, when he painted a Virgin or an Ariadne, or which he copied from the life when he painted the unfortunate Beatrice Cenci. Her jet hair fell in waving luxuriance on her neck and shoulders below her waist; and a small silver plate was bound by a white riband on her forehead. Castruccio could only gaze for a moment on this lovely being; for, turning a supplicating look on her aged friend, she again drew the hood over her face, speaking in so low a tone, that he could not distinguish the words she uttered; the elder lady acted as interpreter, and said: "Beatrice intreats you not to fix the day until to-morrow, and then she hopes, by the grace of God and the Virgin, to name such a one as will bring your enterprize to an happy issue."

Castruccio turned quickly round to see what effect these words would produce upon the bishop; he thought that he saw a slight smile of derision hover on the old man's lip; but he replied: "Be it so; my lord Castruccio, you will accompany my sister, Madonna Marchesana, to her palace; she will disclose to you the secret entrance, and acquaint you with the means by which you may find it, when you return with the marquess Obizzo and his troops."

The assembly broke up; and Castruccio followed Madonna Marchesana and her beautiful companion. His horse was brought to the door; they mounted their white palfreys, and attended by several esquires and pages carrying torches, arrived at a magnificent palace close to the eastern gate of Ferrara. When they had entered, Madonna Marchesana dismissed her servants, and led Castruccio into a room, hung with tapestry, and furnished with the rich and heavy furniture of the age. She lifted up the hangings; and, while

Castruccio supported them, she pushed back a pannel in the wainscot, and discovered a long, dark gallery; then, taking up a torch that lay within, and lighting it at a lamp which hung from the ceiling of the room, she presented it to Beatrice, saying: "Do you, my child, light us, and lead us the way, that success may attend our steps."

A small snow white hand and taper wrist were put out from beneath the capuchin; and Beatrice silently took the torch, and led the way, along the gallery, down several flights of stairs, and then along numerous vaults and corridors, until they arrived at what appeared the end of these subterraneous passages. "You, my lord," said the lady Marchesana, "must help me." She pointed to a large stone, which Castruccio rolled away, and discovered behind it a small, low door. The lady drew back the bolts, and bade Beatrice hide the light, which she did, placing it within a kind of recess in the passage that seemed formed for the purpose of receiving it; the lady then opened the door; and Castruccio, creeping out, found himself in an open country, covered with bushes, and surrounded by marshy land, at some distance from the strong fortifications of the town. Castruccio smiled: "Ferrara is ours!" he cried; and the old lady with a countenance expressive of the greatest delight, said: "I intreat you, my lord, to lay my respectful submission and zealous fidelity at the feet of the marquess Obizzo; tell him the joy and triumph that I feel, in being the humble instrument of restoring him to his sovereignty and inheritance. When you mention the name of the viscountess di Malvezzi he may distrust my professions; since the viscount, my late husband, was his bitter and determined enemy. But he is no more; and I have been brought to a true knowledge of the will of God by this divine girl, this *Ancilla Dei*, as she is truly called, who is sent upon earth for the instruction and example of suffering humanity."

Castruccio listened with astonishment; while the gifted damsel stood, her face covered by her cowl, and her arms crossed over her breast: the eyes of the old lady beamed with joy and pride. "I do not entirely fulfil my commission," she continued, "until I have taught you how you may again discover this place. Do you see those straggling sallows that skirt that stagnant drain, and which, although they appear to be without order, are the clue by which you will be guided thither? Four miles distant from Ferrara, on the right-hand side of the road, you will find a mulberry tree, a poplar, and a cypress, growing close together; strike from the road at that point, and follow the line of sallows, however they may lead, until you come to that where the line ends. You must then mark the drains of the marsh, remembering to follow only those which are bordered by dwarf myrtles, and which at every turn have a cross carved in a low stone on their banks; that line will lead you hither; and you will stop at that cross of wood which you see half buried in the tall grass and bulrushes, until this door is opened for your entrance."

The viscountess di Malvezzi repeated her instructions a second time in the same distinct manner; and, finding that Castruccio fully apprehended them, she led the way back to her subterranean passages; and with quick steps they regained the tapestried apartment. Beatrice remained a moment behind to extinguish the torch; and, when she re-appeared, she had thrown off her capuchin, and shone in the light of her divine beauty. Her dress was of the finest white woollen; and in fashion it partook of the usual dress of the age, and of the drapery of the antient statues: it was confined at her waist by a silken girdle, and fell about her figure in thick and rich folds; a golden cross glittered upon her bosom, on which lay also the glossy ringlets of her hair; on the silver plate bound to her forehead Castruccio could distinguish the words, *Ancilla Dei*. Her black eyes beamed as with inspiration, and the wide sleeves of her vest discovered her white and veined arm, which she threw up in eager gesticulation as she spoke:

"Mother, I promised that to-morrow I would name the day for my sovereign's enterprize; I feel the spirit coming fast upon me; let this noble gentleman inform your revered brother, that to-morrow in the church of St. Anna I shall speak to my countrymen, and in the midst of the people of Ferrara tell in veiled words the moment of their deliverance."

With a light step Beatrice glided out of the room, and the viscountess, not regarding the surprize of Castruccio, said to him: "Fail not, my lord, to convey the message of my Beatrice to the bishop. God has been gracious to us, in bestowing on us his visible assistance through this sacred maiden, who by her more than human beauty, the excellence of her dispositions, and, above all, by her wisdom beyond that of woman, and her prophecies which have ever been fulfilled, demonstrates, even to the unbeliever and the Gentile, that she is inspired by the grace and favour of the blessed Virgin."

[1] A portrait of Christ, said to have been painted by Nicodemus.

CHAPTER II

Parentage of Beatrice.—She is arrested by the Inquisition.

Thus dismissed, Castruccio returned, burning with curiosity and admiration, to the bishop. He delivered the message with which he had been intrusted, and then eagerly asked who this enchanting Beatrice really was, and if it were true that she was an angel descended upon earth for the benefit and salvation of man. The bishop smiled.

"My lord," he replied, "so much have you won my confidence and esteem, that I am willing to satisfy your curiosity on this subject also. But you must recollect, that neither my sister, nor even the lovely girl herself, knows what I shall now reveal, and that I shall tell it you under the most solemn vow of secrecy."

Castruccio readily promised discretion and silence, and the bishop then related the following particulars.

"Have you never heard of a heretic and most dangerous impostor, of the name of Wilhelmina of Bohemia[2]? This woman appeared first in Italy in the year 1289: she took up her residence at Milan, with a female companion, called Magfreda. Outwardly professing the Catholic religion, and conforming in the strictest manner to its rules, she secretly formed a sect, founded on the absurd and damnable belief, that she was the Holy Ghost incarnate upon earth for the salvation of the female sex. She gave out that she was the daughter of Constance, queen of Bohemia; that, as the angel Gabriel had descended to announce the divine conception to the blessed Virgin, so the angel Raphael announced to her mother the incarnation of the Holy Spirit in favour of the female sex; and that she was born twelve months after this heavenly annunciation. Her tenets were intended entirely to supersede those of our beloved Lord Jesus, and her friend Magfreda was to be papess, and to succeed to all the power and privileges of the Roman pontiff. Wilhelmina died in the year 1302 in the odour of sanctity, and was buried in the church of St. Peter at Milan: she had led so holy a life, and kept her heresy so profound a secret, except from her own sect, that she was followed as a saint, and even priests and dignitaries wrote homilies in praise of her piety, her abstinence, and modesty.

"I was at Milan two years after, when the Dominican inquisitors first discovered this lurking pestilence; and the terror and abomination of the discovery filled the town with horror. Magfreda, and her principal follower, Andrea Saramita, were led to prison; the other disciples who threw themselves on the mercy of the priests, being commanded to perform several pilgrimages, and give large alms to the church, were absolved. I had just then become a *Padre*, and filled the confessor's chair: I was young, full of zeal, eloquent in the cause of truth, and tainted by an enthusiastic bigotry against heretics and schismatics. I preached with animation against this new heresy; it appeared to me so impious, so absurd, so terrifically wicked, that I was touched by an holy impulse as I declaimed against its followers. Having thus distinguished myself, the father inquisitors intreated me to use my fervid arguments to persuade the obstinate Magfreda to recant. They had exhausted every reason, and had had recourse even to torture, to convert this woman from her damnable impieties; but she with haughty insolence declared that she was in readiness to perish in the flames, but that her last breath should be spent in the praise of her divine mistress, and an exhortation to her tormentors to repent and believe.

"I was filled with worldly vanity, and fancied that my learned sentences, my anathemas, and eloquent exorcisms could not fail of their desired effect, and that by the aid of God and truth I should be covered with the glory of success in this holy warfare. Thus secure, I entered the dungeon of the heretic: it was a low, damp vault, where she had been confined for several weeks without even straw for her bed. She was kneeling in one corner, praying fervently, and for a moment I stopped to contemplate a heretic, a monster I had never before seen. She was an aged, respectable woman, in the dress of a nun, and with an appearance of sanctity and modesty that astounded me. When she perceived me, she rose, and said with a faint smile: 'Is my condemnation passed? or is a new scene of torture prepared?'

"'Daughter,' I replied, 'I come indeed to torture, not your body, but your mind; to torture it with a knowledge of itself; to hold a mirror before it, wherein you will contemplate its blots and deformities, of which by the grace of the Virgin you may repent and be purified.'

"'Father, you are the master, I a slave, and I am willing to listen. But your benevolent countenance, so different from those to which I have been long accustomed, fills me with such confidence, that I dare hope for your indulgence, when I intreat you to spare yourself a useless labour, and to leave in peace the last hours of my life. I know that I must die; and God and She know how willing I am to expire for Her justification, even in pain and burning: but my spirit is worn, my patience, which I have cherished with determined zeal, as the sacred flame of my religion and the life of my heart, now begins to wane; do not bring on my soul the sins of anger and intolerance;—leave me to prayer, to repentance, and to my hopes of again seeing my beloved mistress, there where there is no sorrow.'

"She spoke with dignity and mildness, so that I felt my spirit subdued; and, although almost angry at the stubbornness of her impiety, I followed her example in speaking with gentleness. Our conversation was long; and the more it continued, the more my animation in the cause of truth, and zeal for the conversion of the heretic, increased. For her manner was so sweet and winning, her words so soft yet firm, that it lay like a sin on my heart that I could not save her from eternal condemnation.

"'You did not know Her,' she cried, 'you never saw my Wilhelmina. Ask those who have seen her, even the vulgar, whose eyes are horn, and whose hearts are stone, whether they were not moved to love and charity, when she passed like an angel among them. She was more beautiful than aught human could be; more gentle, modest and pious than any woman ever was, though she were a saint. Then her words possessed a persuasion that could not be resisted, and her eyes a fire, that betrayed even to the unknowing that the Holy Spirit lived within her.

"'Father, you know not what you ask, when you desire me to leave my faith in her Divinity. I have felt my soul prostrate itself before her; the very blood that vivifies my heart has cried to me, so that, if I had been deaf, I must have heard, that she was more than human. In my dreams I have seen her arrayed in divine light; and even now the sacred radiance that announces her presence fills my dungeon, and bids me for her sake submit with patience to all that ye, her enemies, can inflict.'

"I repeat to you the mad words of Magfreda, that you may judge of the excess of insanity that possessed this unfortunate woman. I combated with the evil spirit within her for eight hours, but in vain; at length I was retiring in despair, when she called me back. I returned with a look of hope, and saw that she was weeping violently and bitterly. As I approached, she seized my hand, and kissed it, and pressed it to her heart, and continued pouring forth, as it were, a fountain of tears. I believed that she was now touched by true repentance, and began to thank divine mercy, when she waved her hand impatiently, beckoning me to be silent. By degrees she calmed her tears; but she was still agitated by passion, as she said: "'Kneel, father, kneel, I intreat you, and by the cross you wear swear secrecy. Alas! if I die, another must perish with me, one whom I have vowed to protect, one whom I love far,—far beyond my own life.'

"She paused, endeavouring to overcome the tears, that, in spite of herself, she shed: I comforted her, and pronounced the desired oath, when she became calmer. 'Father, you are good, benign and charitable; and I do believe that She has manifested Her will in sending you to me in my distress; you, who are so unlike the wolves and harpies that have of late beset me. There is a child—Her child:—but, father, before I reveal further, promise me, swear to me, that she shall be educated in my faith and not in yours.'

"I was indignant at this proposal, and said angrily: 'Woman, think you that I will sacrifice the soul of an infant to your monstrous unbelief and vicious obstinacy? I am a servant of the Lord Jesus, and, believe me, I will never discredit my holy calling.'

"'Must it be so?' she cried; 'yet grant me a few moments to resolve.'

"She knelt down, and prayed fervently for a long time; and then arose with a smiling aspect, saying: 'Father, you wish to convert me; methinks at this moment I could convert you, if indeed faith did not come from God, and not from the human will. She has revealed Her will to me, and by Her command I now confide to you the treasure of my soul.

"'Two years before the death of Wilhelmina, she had a child. I cannot tell you who was the father of this child; for, although I believed that her conception partook of the divinity, she never confirmed my faith, or said aught against it: but with her heavenly smile bade me wait until the hour of knowledge should arrive. I alone knew of the birth of this infant; and it has ever been under my care: it was brought up in a cottage five miles hence by a good woman, who knew not to whom it belonged; and I visited it daily, gazing with wonder on its beauty and intelligence.

"'After its birth Wilhelmina never saw it. She always refused to visit the cottage, or to have it brought to her, but would sit for hours, and listen to my descriptions and praises. I have ever believed that this separation, whatever was its cause, shortened the life of my divine mistress; for she pined, and wept, and faded like a flower unwatered by the dews of heaven. The last words she uttered, were to recommend her infant to my care. I have fulfilled my task, and now, by her command, deliver up my charge to you.

"'A year ago the nurse of the child died; and I took her secretly to my own home, and tended her, and preserved her as her mother had commanded. No love can equal mine for the divinity, her mother: it is a burning affection, an adoration, which no words can express:—I shall never see her more, until we meet in heaven, but I submit with patience to the will of God.

"'When I heard that Andrea Saramita and our other disciples were taken, I was transported with terror for the fate of this infant. I expected every moment to hear the steps of the blood-hounds on the stairs, to seize me, and discover this flower of paradise, which I cherished thus secretly. When suddenly a thought, an inspiration, came over me, and I cried aloud, Better are the wild beast of the forest, and the tempests of heaven, even when they shake us most; better are plague and famine, than man hunting after prey! So I took the infant in my arms, a small purse of gold, and a bag of such provisions as I had in the house; and, it being already dark, I hastened from Milan to the forest that skirts the road to Como: I walked fast, and in two hours arrived at my goal. I knew that one afflicted with leprosy[3] lived in the depth of the forest, a miserable wretch, who with his wooden spoon and platter, collected alms at the road side. Thither I went fearlessly;—mistake me not; this man is not my disciple, he had never seen me before; but I knew not whether the blood-hunters were acquainted with the existence of the divine child, this I knew, that they would not dare seek her in a leper's dwelling. I dreaded not the contagion; *for is not her mother above all the saints in heaven?*

"'I wandered long among the tangled paths of the wood, ere I could discover his hut; the babe slept, cherished near my heart, which bled with anguish. To me in all the world there existed but this little creature; the earth seemed to reel under me; yet still I felt her warm breath upon my bosom, and heard the regular heaving of her gentle breast. At length I found the cavern of the leper: it was half-built in the earthy hill against which it rested, and half of the boughs of trees plastered with mud, which was hardened in the sun; black, dilapidated, and filthy, it was worse than a manger for the reception of my poor innocent.

"'The wretched possessor of this sty slept on his miserable straw as I entered. I roused him, put gold into his hand, and, placing food before him, I said— Protect this child, and God will reward you. Feed it, wash it, and above all keep it from the sight of man: deliver it not except to one who may come to ask for it in the name of the Holy Wilhelmina. In one month I hope to return for it, and will reward you as you have obeyed my charge.—I then, with a heart bursting with agony, embraced the daughter of my Wilhelmina for the last time: I blest her, and tore myself away.

"'I have now been five weeks imprisoned, and I dread lest the leper should have thrust her from his abode. Will you not, father, preserve and love this child?'

"The discourse of Magfreda moved me strangely. I felt a wonder, a pity, an excess of commiseration, I could not express: but kissing the cross I wore, I said: 'Listen to me, unhappy woman, while I swear never to desert this innocent; and may God so help me, as I keep my faith!'

"Magfreda poured forth warm and joyful thanks; then, with a heavy heart, I recommended her to the mercy of God, and left her dungeon.

"As soon as I could tear myself from the questions and childish curiosity of the inquisitors, I hastened to the place that Magfreda had indicated. In the tumult of my soul, I only thought of the danger of the lovely babe in the hands of this outcast of man and nature. I was possessed with a passionate sense of pity, which I cannot now explain, but for which I do not reproach myself; at length, about four miles from the town, I heard the sound of the beggar as he struck his platter with his spoon in token of his wants, and I turned aside from the road to seek him. At that moment the spirit of God almost deserted me, and I was overcome by fear—the fear of disease, and a nameless horror at the expectation of meeting one whom all wholesome life had deserted: but I made the sign of the cross, and approached. The wretch was seated under a tree eating some crusts of bread; miserable, filthy, deformed, his matted hair hung over his eyes and his ragged beard half concealed the lower part of his visage; yet there was to be seen a savage eye, and an appearance of brutal ferocity, that almost staggered me. I made a sign that he should not approach, and he dropped on his knees, and began to gabble *pater-nosters*, so that the word that God himself had spoken seemed the jargon of the devil. I stopt at some distance from him: 'Bring me,' I cried, 'to the child who was confided to you in the name of Wilhelmina of Bohemia.'

"The wretch, who had almost forgotten human speech, jumped up, and led the way among the tangled underwood, along savage paths, overgrown with rank herbage, and bestrewn with stones, till we came to his miserable hut,—a low, dark, squalid den, which I dared not enter; 'Bring me the child,'—I cried.

"Oh; it was a woful sight, and one which to death I shall remember, to see this child, this morning star of beauty and exceeding brightness, with eyes shining with joy, rosy lips melted into the softest smiles, her glossy hair strewn upon her lovely neck, her whole form glowing with the roseate hues of life, led by the leper from his hut; his body wrapt in a ragged blanket, his grizzly hair stretched stiffly out, and his person and face loathsome beyond words to describe. The lovely angel took her hand from his, and coming up to me, said: 'Take me to mamma; lead me from this ugly place to mother.'

"This was Beatrice; and need I say how much I have ever loved this hapless girl, and cherished her, and tried to save her from the fate to which her destiny has hurried her?

"I returned to Milan, and found that in the morning, while I had been absent, Magfreda had been burnt, and her ashes scattered to the winds, so that I had become this poor babe's only guardian. I placed her under the care of a pensioner of the church in the neighbourhood of Milan; and when I was promoted to the see of Ferrara, I brought her with me, and intreated my sister to receive her, and cherish her as her own. The lovely little being won all hearts, and Marchesana soon became attached to her with maternal fondness. She was educated in the Holy Catholic faith; and I hoped that, untainted by her mother's errors, she would lead an unblamed and peaceful life, unmarked and unknown; God has ordered it otherwise.

"Beatrice was always an extraordinary child. When only six and seven years of age, she would sit alone for hours, silently contemplating; and, when I asked her of what she thought, she would weep, and passionately desire me not to ask her. As she grew older, her imagination developed; she would sing extempore hymns with wild, sweet melody, and she seemed to dwell with all her soul on the mysteries of our religion; she then became communicative, and told me how for hours she meditated upon the works of nature, and the goodness of God, till she was filled with a sentiment that overwhelmed and oppressed her, so that she could only weep and sigh. She intreated me to unfold to her all I knew, and to teach her to read in the sacred book of our religion.

"I was fearful that her ignorance and enthusiasm might lead her astray, since, in her accounts of her meditations, she often said things of God and the angels that were heretical; and I hoped that a knowledge of the truth would calm her mind, and lead her to a saner devotion. But my labours had a contrary effect; the more she heard, and the more she read, the more she gave herself up to contemplation and solitude, and to what I cannot help considering the wild dreams of her imagination. It seemed to me as if her mother's soul had descended into her; but that, regulated by the true faith, she had escaped the damnable heresies of that unhappy woman. She delighted to read, and pretended to explain the prophecies of the sacred writings, and the modern ones of Merlin, the abbot Joachim and Methodius: beside these studies, she grew wonderfully familiar with all vulgar superstitions, holy trees and fountains, lucky and unlucky days, and all the silly beliefs that jugglers and impostors encourage for their own profit. At length she began to prophesy; some of her prophecies were interpreted as true, and since that time her fame has been spread through Ferrara. Her followers are numerous; and my poor sister is the first of her disciples: Beatrice herself is wrapt up in the belief of her own exalted nature, and really thinks herself the *Ancilla Dei*, the chosen vessel into which God has poured a portion of his spirit: she preaches, she prophesies, she sings extempore hymns, and entirely fulfilling the part of *Donna Estatica*[4], she passes many hours of each day in solitary meditation, or rather in dreams, to which her active imagination gives a reality and life which confirm her in her mistakes.

"Thus, my lord, I have revealed the birth of this extraordinary girl, which is unknown to every one else. Why I have done this I can hardly tell; for I have done it without premeditation or foresight. But I am glad that you know the truth; for you seem humane and generous; and I wish to secure another protector for my poor Beatrice, if I were to die, and she fell into any misfortune or disgrace."

Castruccio and the good bishop passed almost the whole night in conversation concerning this wonderful creature; and, when the consul retired to rest, he could not sleep, while the beauty of Beatrice was present to his eyes, and her strange birth and fortunes to his memory. In the morning he went to the church of St. Anna: mass was performed, but he looked in vain for the prophetess;—yet, when the service was finished, and the people assembled in the porch of the church, she appeared among them with her aged protectress at her side. She wore her capuchin of light blue silk, but her cowl was thrown back, and her eyes, black as the darkness which succeeds a midnight flash of lightning, full and soft as the shy antelope's, gleamed with prophetic fire.

She spoke; her words flowed with rich and persuasive eloquence, and her energetic but graceful action added force to her expressions. She reproached the people for lukewarm faith, careless selfishness, and a want of fervour in the just cause, that stamped them as the slaves of foreigners and tyrants. Her discourse was long and continued, with the same flow of words and unabated fervour: her musical voice filled the air; and the deep silence and attention of her numerous auditors added to the solemnity of the scene. Every eye was fixed on her,—every countenance changed as hers changed; they wept, they smiled, and at last became transported by her promises of the good that was suddenly to arise, and of the joy that would then await the constant of heart;—when, as this enthusiasm was at its height, some Dominican inquisitors came forward, surrounded her, and declared her their prisoner. Until that moment Castruccio had observed her only,—her flashing eyes and animated manner; the smiles and then the tears, that, as the sunshine and clouds of an April day, succeeded each other on the heaven of her countenance. But, when the inquisitors surrounded her, her voice was silent, and the mute deference of the multitude was no more. All became clamour and confusion; screams, vociferation, ejaculations and curses burst from every tongue;—they declared that the prophetess, the *Ancilla Dei* should not be torn from them,—she was no heretic,—of what crime had she been guilty?—The inquisitors had with them a guard of Gascon soldiers, and this inflamed the multitude still more; it was plain that her adherence to the party of the marquess Obizzo, and the prophecy of his restoration were her only crimes. The noise of her arrest spread through the town, and all Ferrara flocked to the church of St. Anna; the crowd, transported with rage, seemed prepared to rescue the prisoner, who, silent and resigned, stood as one unconcerned in the animated scene. The people armed themselves with stones, sticks, knives, and axes; the inquisitors sent for a reinforcement of Gascon troops, and every thing appeared to menace violence, and bloodshed, when one of the priests attempted to take the hand of Beatrice as if to lead her away; she looked at him with a steady glance, and he drew back, while she made a sign as if about to speak, and the multitude hushed themselves to silence, and were as still, as when a busy swarm of bees, buzzing and flying about, all at once drop to silence, clinging round their queen, who is the mistress of their motions.

She said, "I appeal to the bishop."

"Yes, to the bishop,—to the good bishop; he is just,—take her to him,—he shall decide the cause."

The inquisitors were prepared to resist this appeal: but the will of the people became a torrent not to be stemmed by them, and it hurried them away. They led the prophetess to the episcopal palace, surrounded by the Gascon soldiery, and followed by an immense multitude, which rent the sky with the cries of their anger and despair.

The bishop received the appeal with deep sorrow. Beatrice stood before him, her arms crossed on her breast, her eyes cast down; but on her face, although the gentlest modesty was depicted, there was no trace of fear; she looked intrepid, yet as if she relied not on her own strength, but on that of another. The inquisitors accused her of being an impostor, a misleader of the people, a dangerous and wicked enthusiast, whom the penitence and solitude of a cloister must cure of her extravagant dreams. They talked long and loud, uninterrupted either by the judge or the prisoner, although the lady Marchesana who stood near could not always restrain her indignation.

At length they were silent; and Beatrice spoke: "You call me an impostor,—prove it! I shrink from no trial, I fear no danger or torture,—I appeal to the *Judgement of God*,—on that I rest the truth or falsehood of my mission."

She looked around her with her flashing eyes and glowing cheeks; she was all loveliness, all softness; yet there was a spirit within her, which elevated her above, although it mingled with the feminine delicacy of her mind and manners, and which inspired all who saw her with reverence and tenderness. But a small part of the multitude had found their way into the hall of the bishop's palace; but these could no longer contain themselves; the *Judgement of God* was a thing suited to their vulgar imaginations, as a strange and tremendous mystery, that excited their awe, their pity, and their admiration: they cried, "God can alone judge of this! let the trial be made!" and their screams overpowered every other sound. The inquisitors joined in the clamour, whether to consent or dissent it was impossible to distinguish; at length the scene became calmer, and the bishop interposed his mild voice, but vainly,—the inquisitors repeated the words, impostor! heretic! madwoman! and Beatrice disdainfully refused all composition. It was finally agreed, that she should be confined for that night in the convent of St. Anna, and on the following morning, under the auspices of the monks of the adjoining monastery, should undergo the *Judgement of God*, to be pronounced guilty or innocent as that should declare.

Both the inquisitors and Beatrice retired in security and triumph, followed by the multitude, who were careless of the dismay but too plainly painted on the faces of the prophetess's friends. The lady Marchesana was in dreadful agitation, fluctuating between her faith in the supernatural powers of Beatrice, and her dread lest the trial should bring ruin upon her: she wept, she laughed, she was in a state approaching to madness; until her brother, bidding her confide in God, soothed her to resignation and some degree of confidence. She then retired to pray, leaving the bishop and Castruccio overwhelmed with pity, horror, and indignation.

Then the old man for the first time gave vent to his sorrow:—"Ill-fated victim! headstrong, foolish girl! what are thy prophecies now? thy inspirations and divine aid? alas! alas! the hand of God is upon thee, born in an evil day of a guilty and impious mother! His wrath wraps thee as a cloud, and thou art consumed beneath it;—my love is as bitter ashes,—my hopes are extinct;—oh, that I had died before this day!"

Castruccio was at first too much confounded to offer consolation; but, when he spoke, and bade his friend not despair, the bishop replied: "My lord, she has won my whole soul, and all my affections; why this is, I know not;—is she not beautiful? and she is as good as she is beautiful. She calls me father, and loves me with the tenderness of a child; day and night I have offered up my prayers to God, not to visit on her the sins of her mother;—for her sake I have fasted and prayed,—but all is vain, and she must perish."

"Not so, father; say not that so lovely a being shall perish under the fangs of these cruel hell-hounds. Do not, I earnestly intreat you, despair: flight! flight is her only safety; father, you have authority, and must save her. I will take charge of her, when she has quitted the walls of the convent, and I will place her in safe and honourable guardianship. Let her fly,—by the sun in heaven she shall escape!"

The bishop remained silent for some time; the same ardent blood did not warm his veins, which boiled in those of Castruccio: he saw all the difficulties; he feared for the success of their scheme; but he resolved to make the attempt. "You are right," said he; "flight is her only safety: yet it will be rather a rape, than a flight; for willingly she will never consent to desert the high character she has chosen to assume. Did you not mark her triumph, when the Judgement of God was agreed upon Mad, wild girl!—Let me consider our plan, and weigh our powers. The abbess is a Guelph; but the abbot of the visiting monastery is a Ghibeline; besides the edicts of the church pronounce against these temptations of God's justice. I will exert myself; and she may be saved."

When night closed in, these two anxious friends, alone and wrapt up from observation, hastened to the monastery. Castruccio remained in the parlour;

and the prelate entered the interior of the convent. He remained two hours; while Castruccio, full of anxiety, continued alone in the parlour, which looked on an interior court with no object to call off his attention, in silent and anxious expectation. He thought of the beauty of the prophetess, her animation and numberless graces, until he almost believed in the divinity of her mission: but he shuddered with horror, when he reflected upon her danger, that her ivory feet should press the burning iron, that, if she fell, she would fall on the hot metal, and expire in misery, while the priests, the accursed, self-constituted distributors of God's justice, would sing hymns of triumph over her untimely and miserable fate;—he felt tears gather in his eyes, and he would have devoted himself for her safety. At length the bishop reappeared, and they silently returned to the palace.

"Well! where is she?" were the first words of Castruccio.

"Safe I hope, I trust that I shall not be deceived. I endeavoured to move the abbot to let her escape; I would have gone to the abbess, whose consent I must have obtained, and have used all the influence my station would have given me with her; but the abbot stopped me;—he assured me that he would take care that no harm befel the devoted victim; he begged me not to ask an explanation;—that he and his monks had the charge of the preparation for the Judgement, and that much was in their power; again and again he assured me that she should receive no injury.

"I do not like this:—she must be protected by falsehood and perjury, a lying and blasphemous mockery of the name of God. The abbot, who was a servant of the Popes at Avignon, laughs at my scruples; and I am obliged to yield. She will be saved, and God, I hope, will pardon our human weaknesses. Let the sin lie on the souls of those blood-hounds, who would pursue to destruction the loveliest creature that breathes upon earth."

[2]See Muratori, *Antichristà Italiane*, No. 60.

[3]This disease was then common in Italy. The person affected with it, was accustomed to retire and dwell in a cave in a forest, from whence he resorted to the road-side, and with beating a wooden spoon upon a platter, demanded alms of travellers, which, when they were retired to a convenient distance, he came and took from a stone upon which it was to be deposited.

[4]These inspired women first appeared in Italy after the twelfth century, and have continued even until our own days. After giving an account of their pretensions, Muratori gravely observes, "We may piously believe that some were distinguished by supernatural gifts, and admitted to the secrets of heaven; but we may justly suspect that the source of many of their

revelations, was their ardent imagination, filled with ideas of religion and piety."

CHAPTER III

Judgement of God.—Revolution of Ferrara.

The old man was gloomy and depressed; he retired early to prayer. Castruccio had not slept the preceding night, and he felt his eyes weighed down, although in mind he was agitated and restless; he slept some hours, starting from feverish dreams, in which Euthanasia and poor Beatrice, alike in danger, alike weeping and imploring his aid, filled him with agony. He was awaked before day-break by the bishop's servant; he repaired to the bed-chamber of the prelate, who was sitting on a couch, with haggard looks, and eyes red and inflamed with watching.

"My dear lord," cried the bishop, "I pray you pardon me that I disturb your rest; I cannot sleep. In two hours this ceremony—this mockery begins. I shall not be there; it becomes not my character to be present at such temptations of God's justice: this is my excuse. But I could not go; I should die if I were to behold Beatrice bound and suffering. Yet, do you go, and come quickly back to tell me of her success;—go, and see, if the abbot keeps his word, and if ever I shall behold my child again."

Castruccio endeavoured to console his unhappy friend; but the strong affection and fears of the good man would listen to no comfort. "Let her be saved," he said, "and I am content; but this doubt, this pause of horrid expectation, is more than I can bear; I love her more than father ever loved a child, and she was mine by every tie;—I feel my very life-strings crack, sometimes I am apprehensive I shall die in the agony of doubt; go, go, my dearest lord, go and return quickly, if you love me!"

The bell of the church now began to toll, and announced that the monks were occupied in the prayers that were to precede the ceremony; Castruccio hurried to the scene. It was to take place in a large square of Ferrara, under the walls of the garden of the convent of St. Anna, and before the gates of the monastery to the care of whose monks the Judgement was intrusted. As Castruccio approached, he found every avenue choked up by the multitude, and the house-tops covered with people,—even on towers, whence the square could only appear a confused speck, the people crowded in eager expectation. He joined a few nobles who were admitted through the garden of the monastery; as he passed the sacred precincts, he saw the chapel filled with the brothers, who were praying, while high mass was performed to sanctify their proceedings, and the eucharist was distributed as a pledge of their truth.

The square presented a busy, but awful scene; the houses, the windows of the monastery, the walls of the convent, were covered by people; some clinging to the posts, and to the walls; fixing their feet upon small protuberances of stone, they hung there, as if they stood on air. A large part of the square had been railed off in a semicircle round the door of the monastery, and outside this the people were admitted, while it was guarded on the inside by Gascon soldiers, that with drawn swords kept in awe the eager spectators, whose fury of hope and fear approached madness: their voices it is true were still, for the solemn tolling of the bell struck them with awe, and hushed them, as the roar of the lion in the forest silences the timid herd; but their bodies and muscles were in perpetual motion; some foamed at the mouth, and others gazed with outstretched necks, and eyes starting from their sockets.

Within this inclosure one part was assigned for the Dominican brothers, who, in their black habits and red crosses, at an early hour occupied their seats, which were raised one above another in the form of a small amphitheatre; another part was assigned to some of the nobles of both sexes, the spectators of this piteous scene. Within this inclosure was another small one, close to the gate of the monastery; it had two corresponding entrances, near one of which a large cross was erected, and near the other a white standard with the words *Agnus Dei* embroidered on it. This inclosure was at first empty, except that in one corner a pile of wood was heaped.

Half an hour passed in tremendous expectation: Castruccio felt sick with dread; the heavy and monotonous tolling of the bell struck on his soul, his head ached, his heart sunk within him. At length the gates of the monastery were thrown open, and a number of monks came forward in procession, carrying lights, and chaunting hymns. They saluted the cross, and then ranged themselves round the outside of the inner inclosure; after a pause of few moments, another party came out with Beatrice in the midst of them; she was wrapt in her capuchin, the cowl drawn over her face; the crowd spoke not as she appeared, but a sound, as of the hollow north-wind among the mighty trees of a sea-like forest, rose from among them; an awful, deep and nameless breath, a sigh of many hearts; she was led to the cross, and knelt down silently before it, while the brothers continued to chaunt alternately the staves of a melancholy hymn.

Then came forth a third party of monks; they bore ploughshares and torches, mattocks and other instruments, that again spread a groan of horror through the multitude. The pyre was lighted; the shares thrown in among the blazing wood; while other monks threw up the soil of the inclosure with their mattocks, forming six furrows, two feet distant one from the other. At length the bell, which had been silent for a few minutes, began again to toll, in signal for the ceremony to begin. At the command of the monks Beatrice arose, and threw off her capuchin; she was drest in a short vest of black stuff, fastened at the waist with a girdle of rope; it was without sleeves, and her fairest arms were crossed on her breast; her black and silken hair was scattered on her shoulders; her feet, whiter than monumental marble, were bare. She did not notice the crowd about her, but prayed fervently: her cheek was pale, but her eyes beamed; and in her face and person there was an indescribable mixture of timidity, with a firm reliance on the aid of a superior power. One of the monks bound her arms, and tied a scarf over her eyes: the shares, white with their excessive heat, were drawn from the fire with large tongs, and the monks crowded round, and fixed them in the furrows; the earth seemed to smoke with the heat as they were laid down.

Then the barrier of the entrance to the inclosure was thrown down; the monks quitted it at the opposite end, and one of them with a loud voice, recommending Beatrice to the justice of God, bade her advance. Every heart beat fast; Castruccio overcome by uncontrolable pity, would have darted forward to save her, but some one held him back; and in a moment, before the second beating of his heart, before he again drew breath, horror was converted to joy and wonder. Beatrice, her eyes covered, her arms bound, her feet bare, passed over the burning shares with a quick light step, and reaching the opposite barrier, fell on her knees, uttering an exclamation of thanksgiving to God. These were the first words she had spoken: they were followed by a long and deafening shout of triumph from the multitude, which now manifested its joy as wildly, as before they had painfully restrained their pity and indignation. They were no longer to be contained by the palings of the inclosures; all was broken through and destroyed; the inquisitors had slunk away; and the Gascon troops galloped off from the ground.

Immediately on the completion of her task, Beatrice had been unbound, and her capuchin was thrown over her; the noble ladies who were present crowded round her; she was silent and collected; her colour indeed was heightened by her internal agitation, and her limbs trembled with the exertion of her fortitude; but she commanded her countenance and spirits, and at least wore the appearance of serenity. She received the congratulations and respectful salutation of her friends with affectionate cordiality; while the air resounded with the triumphant *Te Deum* of the monks, and the people pressed around, awed, but joyful. They endeavoured to touch the garment of the newly declared saint; mothers brought her their sick children; the unhappy intreated for her prayers; and, however bashful and unwilling, she was obliged to bestow her blessing on all around. Suddenly a procession of nuns came forth from the garden-gate of the convent; covered with their long veils, and singing their hymns, they surrounded Beatrice, and led her, attended by the other ladies in company, to their cloisters, where her maternal friend the viscountess Marchesana waited to clasp her in her arms.

Castruccio had already returned to the bishop; yet he came not so quickly, but that the news of the success of his Beatrice, passing from mouth to mouth, had reached him. His first emotions were joy, gratitude, and wonder; but these subsided; and the good old man kneeled humiliated, trembling and penitent, when he considered that God's name had been called on in vain, that his consecrated servants were perjured, and that falsehood was firmly established, on foundations where truth alone ought to rest. He listened to the account of Castruccio with interrupted exclamations and tears; and when it was ended he exclaimed, "This is the most miserable—the happiest day of my life!"

In the evening the palace of the prelate was crowded by his friends, who, knowing the interest he took in Beatrice, came to congratulate him on her victory, and to express their delight that God had thought their town worthy of this manifestation of his grace. The bishop, joyful, but full of shame, listened in silence to their conjectures, exclamations, and long relations of the morning's scene; his heart was glad, but he was angry with himself for feeling pleasure at the triumph of falsehood; and, although a smile played on his lips, a blush spread itself over his aged cheeks.

The viscountess Malvezzi, radiant with delight, and the lovely Beatrice blushing under her newly acquired honours, now entered; the nobles pressed round the prophetess, kissing her hand, and the hem of her garment; while she, modest, half abashed, yet believing in her right to the reverence of her friends, smiled upon all. Castruccio was not among the last of her worshippers; she had never appeared so beautiful; her eyes, sparkling with the light of triumph, were yet half hid by their heavy lids, her cheeks glowing, her graceful person, clothed in her modest garb of white woollen, moved with gestures ever new and beautiful:—she seemed another being from her he had before seen, as inspired, as ethereal, but more lovely.

After the crowd of visitors had retired, a few of the intimate friends who formed the council of the bishop remained; the lady Marchesana invited them immediately to adopt some plan for the entrance of their prince into the city; she continued: "I speak but the words of my child, when I say this; pardon me, saintly Beatrice, that I call you thus. It is sweet to me to fancy that you are my daughter, although I am much unworthy of such a child, and you are the offspring of heaven alone."

Beatrice kissed the hand of her excellent friend with respect and gratitude; the bishop was much troubled at his sister's expression; the remembrancer of her heretic mother, and his prison-scene with Magfreda, was full in his recollection, and he looked up to heaven, as if to ask God to pardon him, and to avert the punishment of deceit from the guileless Beatrice.

One of the nobles present asked the sacred maiden, to name the day when the prince should enter the town. She said in a gentle voice: "My lords, the hour of victory is at hand: the Popes, in despite of their duty, have deserted their sacred city, have relinquished their lawful rule, and would now establish tyranny among us,—it will not be. Four days hence, on the evening of Monday, we shall receive our sovereign, and on the following morning his banner will be unfurled on the battlements of this city."

"On Monday," cried a noble, "my heart misgives me; methinks it is an Ægyptian day; has no one a calendar?"

"It is an Ægyptian day," exclaimed Beatrice, with vivacity; "but the adverse aspect of the stars falls on our adversaries; for us there is joy and victory."

"Monday is an early day," said Castruccio; "but as the holy Beatrice commands, so shall it be. And, my honoured lord, I shall leave you at day-break to-morrow. I shall not see you again, divine prophetess, until I come with your prince, to assert his right. I pray you therefore to bless my arms, and cause, that I may be doubly valiant, approved by one whom heaven has sent us."

Castruccio kneeled to the beautiful girl; he looked up at her with his ardent eyes, his passion-formed lips, and countenance of frank and noble beauty; she blushing placed her hand on his raven hair, and said, "May God bless and prosper thee and thy cause!"—Then, beckoning her aged friend, she silently saluted the company, and withdrew, abashed, confused, but her heart beating with a new and strange sense of pleasure.

The plan for the entrance of the marquess was now arranged. On the night of the fourth of August he was to pass Lago Scuro, and halt with his troops, at the path which led to the secret entrance to the Malvezzi palace. The marquess, Castruccio, and a small party were to enter the house of the viscountess; and Galeazzo to lead the greater part of the remainder to the gates of the town by day-break the following morning; a part was to remain as a *corps de reserve*, if the small escort of the marquess should prove insufficient to force the opening of the gates, and the entrance of Galeazzo. In that case this more numerous troop was to enter the city through the house of the viscountess, and bring the necessary succour to their prince.

The assembly then broke up; and Castruccio, wearied by the events of the day, fatigued with want of rest, his spirits sinking after their relaxation from the powerful excitements they had sustained, retired early to repose. He took an affectionate leave of the good old prelate, who charged him with many messages of fidelity and attachment to his prince.

The dawn of day beheld Castruccio on the road to Rovigo. The wide plain of Lombardy awoke to life under the rising sun. It was a serene morning; the cloudy mists that settled on the horizon, received the roseate glories of the rising sun, and the soft clouds of gold and pink that awaited his appearance in the east, would have pictured forth to a Grecian eye the chariot of Aurora, or the golden gates which the Hours threw back as Phœbus entered upon his diurnal path.

And does the beauteous prophetess seek her tower to behold the glories of the morn? Beatrice is on the *donjon* of the palace; and it is true that her eyes are directed towards the rising sun; but there is a casque which flashes under its first beams, a horseman who gallops away from Ferrara, whose form her eyes strain to behold, even when he appears only as a black spot in the distance. She leans her cheek upon her hand, and, lost in meditation, she, most unfortunate, mistakes for the inspirations of Heaven the wild reveries of youth and love: but still her heart was hidden even from herself by a veil she did not even wish to throw aside. She felt gently agitated, but happy; a kind of Elysian happiness, that trembled at change, and wished only for a secure eternity of what it was.

Castruccio was hailed with joy by his friends at Rovigo; and, when the intelligence he brought was heard, every voice was busy in congratulation, every hand in preparation. The knights assisted the squires in furbishing their arms, and securing the various joints and fastenings of their heavy armour, in looking that the trusty blade of the sword was well fixed in the pummel, in selecting the stoutest lances, and in attending to all the other equipments of war; while the fair hands of the ladies prepared the scarfs, which, tied over the hearts of their knights, would preserve them from every wound. No thought of danger and death,—this was to be rather a tournament, wherein with blunted lances they tilted for a sovereignty; and the idea of the Pope, and of their priest-ridden opponents and their foreign guards excited derision alone.

The sun set on the fourth day, and the troops of the marquess Obizzo to the number of four hundred were drawn out before the gates of Rovigo. The expedition was ordered as it had been arranged; and in the depth of night the viscountess, opening the low door of her secret entrance, found the marquess, Castruccio, and their followers, waiting in silence round the short half-buried cross on the marshy moor. A few whispered words of recognition having been spoken, she led them along her galleries, and up the staircase to the inhabited rooms of the palace, lifting up the tapestry of the first apartment; Castruccio did not again know the old, neglected chamber with its decaying furniture. It was hung with silk, festooned with flowers, and lighted by a hundred wax lights; a table was spread with wines, and fruits, and sweetmeats, and other more substantial refreshments; several couches also were placed round the room for the convenience of those who wished to repose.

The viscountess with courtly grace welcomed the marquess to her palace. "My lord," she said, "for a few hours you must be imprisoned in this apartment; I have endeavoured to decorate your poor dungeon to the best of my power, and indeed shall ever hold this room honoured, since it affords refuge and protection to my sovereign."

The old lady received the marquess's heartfelt thanks, and then retired satisfied, to recount to Beatrice the arrival of her guests, and the whispered enquiry of Castruccio concerning the health of the prophetess. But, although she had gilt their cage, the hours passed heavily to the imprisoned chiefs; they watched the stars as they still burned brightly in the sky, and almost uttered a cry of joy when they first perceived them, one by one, fading in the morning light. At length the steps of men were heard about the streets; and the horses which the bishop had provided for the troop came to the door of the palace. The trampling of these horses as they were led to their destination, attracted a small crowd along with them; and, when the strange knights mounted them, and advanced in slow procession along the streets, the crowd increased, and the name of the marquess was whispered, while every one gazed in wonder. At length, when the troop had reached the principal street of Ferrara, they put their horses to the gallop, and raising the Ghibeline war-cry, rode through the town calling on the people to join them, and invoking downfal to the foreign tyrants: a band of citizens, who had been already prepared, obeyed the summons, and they were followed by others, who espoused the party of the prince in their hearts, and joyfully aided his restoration.

The trampling of the steeds, the clash of arms, as the knights struck their shields with their spears, the war-cry of the troops, and the *vivas* of the crowd, awoke the papal governor, who called out the Gascon soldiery. But it was too late; the marquess reached the gate of the town, put the sentinels to flight, and admitted Galeazzo into the city: then, joined by all the nobility of Ferrara, he rode towards the palace of the governor. The Gascons were drawn up in the great square of the town, but they were unable to withstand the first onset of Obizzo's party; they fled, and shut themselves up in Castel Tealdo, the fortress of the town, where they were at least safe from sudden attack. The marquess drew his troops around, and threw up his works to prevent their egress; and, leaving to his principal captain the care of the siege, returned to his palace to receive the congratulations of his delighted subjects.

Now joy was the order of the day; the Italians, who had been intrusted with the charge of some of the gates of the town, brought the keys to the feet of their sovereign; the others were broken open; every magistrate brought in his resignation, and many of them petitions for mercy; and lying traitors, who assured him that their faith had never been broken, crowded to the presence-chamber. His throne was erected in the great square, covered with the richest cloth, and surmounted by a magnificent canopy; the troops were marshalled before him, the standards brought and lowered to his feet. A deputation of the noblest counts and knights of Ferrara were sent to convoy the caroccio[5] to the throne of the prince. They went to the cathedral; and the monks led it forth, adorned with its splendid trappings and standards, the gold cross and white flag of the Popes waving above all. They yoked to it four beautiful dove coloured oxen, on whom they cast rich trappings of scarlet cloth; and then, to the sound of trumpets, surrounded by the knights, and followed by a procession of priests singing a *Te Deum*, it was drawn to the square before the throne of Obizzo; then with a triumphant flourish, the standard of the Pope was lowered, and that of the house of Este raised to its ancient eminence. Festivities of every kind followed this joyful event, triumphant festivities, untarnished with blood; for few of the subjects of the marquess were hostile to his return, and these either went into voluntary exile, or joined the refugees in Castel Tealdo.

[5] The Caroccio was introduced after the tenth century. It was a large car, painted red, adorned with numerous standards, the spoils of vanquished enemies, and surmounted by the banner of the *commune* to which it belonged. It made a considerable figure in the wars of Frederic Barbarossa. Its loss was an indelible disgrace, and its capture the greatest of triumphs.

CHAPTER IV

Fall of Beatrice.

Castruccio was no inactive partaker in this busy scene. But, after the combat was finished, and he perceived that Obizzo was engaged in acts of peaceful sovereignty alone, he hastened to the palace of the bishop; for he was painfully surprised in not seeing him among the nobles who waited on the prince. The old man was ill: he had been dreadfully agitated by the scenes of the preceding days, and his health for a while sunk under it. Castruccio was introduced into his chamber, where he lay peacefully sleeping on a magnificent couch, his adopted child, the lovely Beatrice, watching before him, who, when she beheld Castruccio, blushed deeply, while, in spite of every effort, a smile of delight spread itself over her expressive countenance.

"He is not very ill," she said in a low voice, in answer to Castruccio's enquiries; "the fever has left him entirely; he is weak, but recovering. He sleeps sweetly now: look at him; at his reverend grey hairs strewn over his naked temples; look at his eyes, sunken with age, yet, when open, beaming with benevolence and affection: look what a gentle smile there is upon his pale lips; there he sleeps, affection, benevolence, matchless virtue, and excelling wisdom, all cradled by the baby Sleep; I have been contemplating him for more than an hour; he draws his breath as regularly as a sleeping infant who has sucked its fill, and his heart heaves slowly, but calmly. It is a heavenly sight to look on the repose of this good old man; it calms wild passion, and sheds the fresh dew of healthful meditation over the strange reveries of youth."

She spoke in a whisper; but her countenance was all animation. The old man moved; and, pressing her finger on her lips, she paused. "Beatrice, my child," he said, "I have slept long and soundly, and feel quite well. Who is that stranger? does he bring news from the marquess? Aye, I remember this is the day,—I am strangely confused; I recollect now that I heard of his success before I slept."

"Father, it is my lord Castruccio, who, after having reinstated our prince in his sovereignty, visits your sick chamber."

Castruccio remained several hours conversing with the bishop; he gave him an account of the action of the morning, and Beatrice listened with her whole soul in her eyes; yet, attentive as she was to the narration, she watched with sweet earnestness her sick friend, turning her looks from him to the animated face of Castruccio; and again, as she crept near her adoptive father, she adjusted some pillow, or performed some little office that marked her earnest observation.

"How beautiful she is!" thought Castruccio, "and what will become of her?" he fixed his eyes on the silver plate on her forehead. "Yes, she is the *Ancilla Dei*, a maiden vowed to God and chastity; yet her eyes seem penetrated with love; the changeful and blooming colours of her face, her form, which is all that imagination can conceive of perfect, appear not like those of a cloistered nun. Ah! Beatrice, if you would be sacred to your God, you ought to hide your surpassing loveliness with thick veils, behind treble grates. But she is a prophetess; something more than human;—a character unapproachable even in thought."

Thus Castruccio tried to disentangle his perplexed thoughts, still looking on the maiden, who, suddenly raising her eyes, and meeting his which were fixed on her silver plate, blushed even till the tips of her fingers became a rosy red; and then, complaining in an hesitating voice, that the plate hurt her brow, she untied it; while her silken hair, no longer confined, fell on her neck.

Thus many hours passed, and when at length the prophetess retired, it was to feverish meditation, and thoughts burning with passion, rendered still more dangerous from her belief in the divine nature of all that suggested itself to her mind. She prayed to the Virgin to inspire her; and, again giving herself up to reverie, she wove a subtle web, whose materials she believed heavenly, but which were indeed stolen from the glowing wings of love. Kneeling, her eyes raised to heaven, she felt the same commotion in her soul, which she had felt before, and had recognised as divine inspiration; she felt the same uncontrolable transport and burst of imaginative vision, which she believed to flow immediately from the invisible ray of heaven-derived prophecy. She felt her soul, as it were, fade away, and incorporate itself with another and a diviner spirit, which whispered truth and knowledge to her mind, and then slowly receding, left her human nature, agitated, joyful, and exhausted;—these were her dreams,—alas! to her they were realities.

The following morning she again met Castruccio in the chamber of the bishop. She now looked upon him fearlessly; and, if the virgin modesty of her nature had not withheld her, her words would have been as frank as she innocently believed them to be inspired. But, although she was silent, her looks told that she was changed. Her manner the day before had been soft, concentrated, and retiring; now she was unconstrained; her eyes sparkled, and a joyous expression dwelt in every feature. Her manner towards her guardian was endearing, nor was the affectionate modulation of her voice different when she addressed his guest: Castruccio started to hear it. It reminded him of the accents of Euthanasia, whom for a while he had forgotten; and, looking at Beatrice, he thought, "How lovely she is, and yet how unlike!"

Several days passed thus; Beatrice became embarrassed; it seemed as if she wished to speak to Castruccio, and yet dared not: when she approached, she blushed, and again drew back, and would again seek him, but again vainly. She had framed the mode of her address, conned and reconned the words she should say; but, when an opportunity occurred to utter them, her voice failed her, the memory of what she was about to utter deserted her, and it was not until the approach of a third person took from her the possibility of speaking, that speech again returned, and the lost occasion was uselessly lamented. At night she sought the counsels of heaven, and gave herself up to her accustomed extasies; they always told her the same things, until to her bewildered and untamed mind it seemed as if the spirit that had power over her, reprimanded her hesitation, her little trust in the promises of heaven, and her reluctance to follow the path it pointed out.

"Surely, oh! most certainly," she thought, "thus I am commanded by the Power who has so often revealed his will to me. Can I penetrate his hidden designs? can I do more than execute his decrees? did I not feel thus, when with prophetic transport I foretold distant events that surely came to pass? when I foresaw yet afar off the death of Lorenzo, that lovely child blooming in health, when every one called me a false prophet? And yet he died. And now, the marquess's return? nay, am I not approved by heaven? did I not escape from the malice of my enemies through its miraculous interposition? Oh! I will no longer scan with presumptuous argument, purposes that are ruled by mightier hands than mine; I will resign myself to the guidance of what has ever conducted me aright, and which now points out the path to happiness."

The next morning, her cheeks flushed, her eyes weighed down, trembling and abashed, she sought Castruccio. It is impossible that there should not have been much tenderness in his manner towards this lovely girl; her history, her strange and romantic contemplations and impulses, and the great intimacy which had arisen between them, were sufficient for this. He regarded her also as a nun; and this made him feel less restraint in the manner of his address, since he feared not to be misconstrued; while at the same time it gave an elevation and unusual tone to his ideas concerning her, that made him watch her every motion with interest. She now approached; and he said playfully; "Where is thy mark, prophetess? art thou no longer the *Maiden of God?* For some days thou hast cast aside the hallowed diadem."

"I still have it," she replied; "but I have dismissed it from my brow; I will give it you; come, my lord, this evening at midnight to the secret entrance of the viscountess's palace." Saying these words, she fled to hide her burning blushes in solitude, and again to feel the intoxicating delusions that led her on to destruction.

Castruccio came. If it were in human virtue to resist the invitation of this angelic girl, his was not the mind, strictly disciplined to right, self-examining and jealous of its own integrity that should thus weigh its actions, and move only as approved by conscience. He was frank and noble in his manner; his nature was generous; and, though there lurked in his heart the germ of an evil-bearing tree, it was as yet undeveloped and inanimated; and, in obeying the summons of Beatrice, he passively gave himself up to the strong excitements of curiosity and wonder.

He went again and again. When the silent night was spread over every thing, and the walls of the town stood black and confused amidst the overshadowing trees, whose waving foliage was diversified by no gleam of light, but all was formless as the undistinguishable air; or if a star were dimly seen, it just glistened on the waters of the marsh, and then swiftly the heavy web of clouds hid both star and water; when the watch dogs were mute, unawakened by the moon, and the wind that blew across the plain alone told to the ear the place of the trees; when the bats and the owls were lulled by the exceeding darkness; it was on such nights as these, that Castruccio sought the secret entrance of the viscountess's palace, and was received by the beautiful Beatrice, enshrined in an atmosphere of love and joy.

She was a strange riddle to him. Without vow, without even that slight shew of distrust which is the child of confidence itself; without seeking the responsive professions of eternal love, she surrendered herself to his arms. And, when the first maiden bashfulness had passed away, all was deep tenderness and ardent love. Yet there was a dignity and a trusting affection in her most unguarded moments, that staggered him: a broken expression would sometimes fall from her lips, that seemed to say that she believed him indissolubly hers, which made him start, as if he feared that he had acted with perfidy; yet he had never solicited, never promised,—what could she mean? What was she? He loved her as he would have loved any thing that was surpassingly beautiful; and, when these expressions, that intimated somewhat of enduring and unchangeable in their intercourse, intruded themselves, they pained and irritated him: he turned to the recollection of Euthanasia, his pure, his high-minded, and troth-plight bride;—she seemed as if wronged by such an idea; and yet he hardly dared think her purer than poor Beatrice, whose soul, though given up to love, was imbued in its very grain and texture with delicate affections and honourable feelings; all that makes the soul and living spark of virtue. If she had not resisted the impulses of her soul, it was not that she wanted the power; but that, deluded by the web of deceit that had so long wound itself about her, she believed them, not only lawful, but inspired by the special interposition of heaven.

Poor Beatrice! She had inherited from her mother the most ardent imagination that ever animated a human soul. Its images were as vivid as reality, and were so overpowering, that they appeared to her, when she compared them to the calm sensations of others, as something superhuman; and she followed that as a guide, which she ought to have bound with fetters, and to have curbed and crushed by every effort of reason. Unhappy prophetess! the superstitions of her times had obtained credit for, and indeed given birth to her pretensions, and the compassion and humanity of her fellow creatures had stamped them with the truth-attesting seal of a miracle. There is so much life in love! Beatrice was hardly seventeen, and she loved for the first time; and all the exquisite pleasures of that passion were consecrated to her, by a mysteriousness and delusive sanctity that gave them tenfold zest. It is said, that in love we idolize the object; and, placing him apart and selecting him from his fellows, look on him as superior in nature to all others. We do so; but, even as we idolize the object of our affections, do we idolize ourselves: if we separate him from his fellow mortals, so do we separate ourselves, and, glorying in belonging to him alone, feel lifted above all other sensations, all other joys and griefs, to one hallowed circle from which all but his idea is banished; we walk as if a mist or some more potent charm divided us from all but him; a sanctified victim which none but the priest set apart for that office could touch and not pollute, enshrined in a cloud of glory, made glorious through beauties not our own. Thus we all feel during the entrancing dream of love; and Beatrice, the ardent, affectionate Beatrice, felt this with multiplied power: and, believing that none had ever felt so before, she thought that heaven itself had interfered to produce so true a paradise. If her childish dreams had been full of fire, how much more vivid and overpowering was the awakening of her soul when she first loved! It seemed as if some new and wondrous spirit had descended, alive, breathing and panting, into her colder heart, and gave it a new impulse, a new existence. Ever the dupe of her undisciplined thoughts, she cherished her reveries, believing that heavenly and intellectual, which was indebted for its force to earthly mixtures; and she resigned herself entire to her visionary joys, until she finally awoke to truth, fallen, and for ever lost.

In the mean time peace was entirely restored to Ferrara: on the fifteenth of August Castel Tealdo surrendered, and the Pope's governor, with his foreign guard, quitted the territories of the marquess of Este. Galeazzo Visconti returned to Milan, but still Castruccio lingered: he wished to go; he found himself out of place as a dangling courtier in the train of Obizzo; but how could he leave Beatrice? What did she expect or wish? The passionate tenderness that she evinced, could not be an ephemeral spark of worthless love; and how often did the *We,* she used in talking of futurity, make him pause when he wished to speak of their separation! She seemed happy; her words flowed in rich abundance, and were adorned with various imagery and with delicate thoughts, shewing that her soul, at rest from fear, wandered as it was wont amidst the wilds of her imagination. He found her untaught, undisciplined, but so sincere, so utterly forgetful of self, so trusting, that he dared not speak that, which each day shewed more clearly would be as a dagger to her heart. A thousand times he cursed himself for having mistaken her, and imagining, inspired as she believed herself to be, that her actions and feelings had not been dictated by the loftiest impulses. But the time arrived, when he was obliged to undeceive her; and the hand, that tore away the ties her trusting heart had bound round itself, at the same time tore away the veil which had for her invested all nature, and shewed her life as it was—naked and appalling.

They sat in her apartment at the Malvezzi palace; she radiant, beautiful, and happy; and, twining her lovely arms around Castruccio, she said: "The moon will set late to-morrow-night, and you must not venture here; and indeed for several nights it will spread too glaring a beam. But tell me, are you become a citizen of Ferrara? They averred that you were the head of a noble city; but I see they must have been mistaken, or the poor city must totter strangely, so headless as your absence must make it. How is this, my only friend? Are you not Antelminelli? Are we not to go to Lucca?"

Castruccio could not stand the questioning of her soft yet earnest eyes; he withdrew himself from her arms, and taking her hands in his, kissed them silently. "How is my noble lord?" she repeated, "have you had ill news? are you again banished? that cannot be, or methinks my heart would have told me the secret. Yet, if you are, be not unhappy:—your own Beatrice, with prophetic words, and signs from heaven that lead the multitude, will conduct you to greater glory and greater power than you before possessed. My gentle love, you have talked less about yourself, and about your hopes and desires, than I should have wished:—Do not think me a foolish woman, tied to an embroidery frame, or that my heart would not beat high at the news of your success, or that with my whole soul I should not enter into your plans, and tell you how the stars looked upon your intents. In truth my mind pants for fitting exertion; and, in being joined to thee, dearest love, I thought that I had found the goal for which heaven had destined me. Nay, look not away from me; I do not reproach thee; I know that, in finding thee, in being bound to thy fate, mine is fulfilled; and I am happy. Now speak—tell me what has disturbed thy thoughts."

"Sweetest Beatrice, I have nothing to tell; yet I have for many days wished to speak; for in truth I must return to Lucca."

The quick sensations of Beatrice could not be deceived. The words of Castruccio were too plain; she looked at him, as if she would read the secret in his soul,—she did read it:—his downcast eyes, confused air, and the words he stammered out in explanation, told her every thing. The blood rushed to her face, her neck, her hands; and then as suddenly receding, left even her lips pale. She withdrew her arms from the soft caress she had bestowed; playfully she had bound his head with her own hair and the silken strings entangled with his; she tore her tresses impatiently to disengage herself from him; then, trembling, white, and chilled, she sat down, and said not a word. Castruccio looked on with fear; he attempted consolation.

"I shall visit thee again, my own Beatrice; for a time we must part;—the viscountess—the good bishop—you cannot leave them,—fear not but that we shall meet again."

"We shall meet again!" she exclaimed with a passionate voice; "Never!"

Her tone, full of agitation and grief, sunk into the soul of Castruccio. He took her hand; it was lifeless; he would have kissed her; but she drew back coldly and sadly. His words had not been those of the heart; he had hesitated and paused: but now compassion, and the memory of what she had been, awoke his powers, and he said warmly, and with a voice whose modulations seemed tuned by love: "You mistake me, Beatrice; indeed you do. I love you;—who could help loving one so true, so gentle, and so trusting?—we part for a while;—this is necessary. Does not your character require it? the part you act in the world? every consideration of honour and delicacy:—Do you think that I can ever forget you? does not your own heart tell you, that your love, your caresses, your sweet eyes, and gentle words, have woven a net which must keep me for ever? You will remain here, and I shall go; but a few suns, a few moons, and we shall meet again, and the joy of that moment will make you forget our transient separation."

How cold were these words to the burning heart of the prophetess; she, who thought that Heaven had singled out Castruccio to unite him to her, who thought that the Holy Spirit had revealed himself to bless their union, that, by the mingled strength of his manly qualities, and her divine attributes, some great work might be fulfilled on earth; who saw all as God's command, and done by his special interposition; to find this heavenly tissue swept away, beaten down, and destroyed! It was to his fortunes, good or bad, that she had bound herself, to share his glory or soothe his griefs; and not to be the mistress of the passing hour, the distaff of the spinning Hercules. It was her heart, her whole soul she had given; her understanding, her prophetic powers, all the little universe that with her ardent spirit she grasped and possessed, she had surrendered, fully, and without reserve; but alas! the most worthless part alone had been accepted, and the rest cast as dust upon the winds. How in this moment did she long to be a winged soul, that her person heedlessly given, given only as a part of that to the whole of which he had an indefeasible right, and which was now despised, might melt away from the view of the despiser, and be seen no more! The words of her lover brought despair, not comfort; she shook her head in silence; Castruccio spoke again and again; but many words are dangerous where there is much to conceal, and every syllable he uttered laid bare some new forgery of her imagination, and shewed her more and more clearly the harsh reality. She was astounded, and drank in his words eagerly, though she answered not; she was impatient when he was silent, for she longed to know the worst; yet she dared not direct the course of his explanations by a single enquiry: she was as a mother, who reads the death-warrant of her child on the physician's brow, yet blindly trusting that she decyphers ill, will not destroy the last hope by a question. Even so she listened to the assurances of Castruccio, each word being a fresh assurance of her misery, yet not stamping the last damning seal on her despair.

At length grey dawn appeared; she was silent, motionless and wan; she marked it not; but he did; and rising hastily he cried, "I must go, or you are lost; farewel, Beatrice!"

Now she awoke, her eyes glared, her lovely features became even distorted by the strength of her agony,—she started up—"Not yet, not yet—one word more! Do you—love another?"

Her tone was that of command;—her flashing eyes demanded the truth, and seemed as if they would by their excessive force strike the falsehood dead, if he dared utter it: he was subdued, impelled to reply:—

"I do."

"Her name?"

"Euthanasia."

"Enough, I will remember that name in my prayers. Now, go! seek not to come again; the entrance will be closed; do not endeavour to see me at the house of the bishop; I shall fly you as a basilisk, and, if I see you, your eyes will kill me. Remember these are my words; they are as true, as that I am all a lie. It will kill me; but I swear by all my hopes never to see you more. Oh, never, never!"

She again sank down pale and lifeless, pressing her hands upon her eyes, as if the more speedily to fulfil her vow. Castruccio dared stay no longer, he fled as the dæmon might have fled from the bitter sorrows of despoiled Paradise; he left her aghast, overthrown, annihilated.

He quitted Ferrara that day. He was miserable: careless of the road, he sought solitude alone. Before night he was among the wild forests of the Apennines,—and there he paused; he was surrounded by the dark pine-forests that sung above him, covered by a night which was cloudy and unquiet, for the swift wind drove the rack along the sky, and moaned, and howled; while the lightnings of a distant storm, faint, but frequent, displayed the savage spot on which he rested. He threw himself from his horse, and abandoned himself to sorrow: it stung him to reflect, that he was the cause of sharpest pain to one who loved him; and the excuses he fondly leaned upon before his explanation, broke as a reed under the wild force of Beatrice's despair. He had heard her story, he knew her delusions, and ought not to have acted towards her, as to a fellow-being who walked in the same light as himself, and saw objects dressed in the same colours: a false sun made every thing deceptive for her eyes,—and he knew it.

Yet what could he now do? Go again to Beatrice? Wherefore? What could he say? but one word—"forget me!" And that was already said. His early vows, his deepest and his lasting hopes, were bound up in Euthanasia: she depended on him alone; she had no father, no relation, none to love but him. She had told him that she gave up her soul to him, and had intreated him not to cast aside the gift. Beatrice had never demanded his faith, his promise, his full and entire heart; but she believed that she had them, and the loss sustained by her was irretrievable.

Yet she would soon forget him: thus he reasoned; hers was one of those minds ever tossed like the ocean by the tempest of passion; yet, like the ocean, let the winds abate, and it subsides, and quickly again becomes smiling. She had many friends; she was loved, nay, adored, by all who surrounded her: utter hopelessness of ever seeing him again would cause her to forget him; her old ideas, her old habits would return, and she would be happy. His interference alone could harm her; but she, the spoiled child of the world, would weep out her grief on some fond and friendly bosom, and then again laugh and play as she was wont.

He spent the following day and night among these forests; until the tempest of his soul was calmed, and his thoughts, before entangled and matted by vanity and error, now flowed loose, borne on by repentance, as the clinging weeds of a dried-up brook are spread free and distinct by the re-appearance of the clear stream. He no longer felt the withering look of Beatrice haunt even his dreams; it appeared to him that he had paid the mulct of remorse and error; the impression of her enchantments and of her sorrows wore off; and he returned with renewed tenderness to Euthanasia, whom he had wronged; and, in the knowledge that he had shamed her pure lessons, he felt a true and wholesome sorrow, which was itself virtue. Yet he dared not go back to her; he dared not meet her clear, calm eye; and he felt that his cheek would burn with shame under her innocent gaze. He suddenly remembered his engagement to visit Pepi, the old Ghibeline politician, who, without honesty or humanity, snuffed up the air of self-conceit, and who, thus inflated, believed himself entitled to cover others with the venom of sarcasm and contempt.

"Yes, old fox!" he cried, "I will unearth you, and see if there is aught in your kennel worth the labour. Methinks you would give out as if gold were under the dirt, or that power and wisdom lurked beneath your sheep-skin and wrinkles; but believe me, my good friend, we Italians, however base our politics may be, are not yet low enough to feed from a trough with you for the driver."

The recollection of something so low and contemptible as Benedetto of Cremona, relieved Castruccio from a load of dissatisfaction and remorse. Comparing Pepi with himself, not directly, but by inference of infinite contempt, he felt that he could again unabashed raise his eyes. This was not well; far better was the blush of humiliation which covered him in comparing his soiled purposes and strayed heart to something high and pure, than the ignoble heavings of self-consequence in matching himself with such a blotted specimen of humanity as Pepi. So, as we are wont, when we return from the solitude of self-examination to the company of fellow-sinners, he twisted up again the disentangled tresses of his frank and sincere thoughts into the million-knotted ties of the world's customs and saintly-looking falsehoods; and, leaving the woods of the Apennines, something wiser in self-knowledge, and but little improved in generous virtue, and the government of his passions, he put spurs to his horse, and turned his steps towards Cremona.

CHAPTER V

Visit to Pepi at Cremona.

It was on the evening of the tenth of September that Castruccio arrived at the bridge which Pepi had indicated. No one was there, except an old woman spinning with a distaff, who from her age and wrinkles might have served for a model of the eternal Fates; for her leathern and dry, brown skin, did not seem formed of the same frail materials as the lily cheek of a high-bred dame. She looked full at Castruccio; so that he laughing asked her, whether she would tell him his fortune.

"Aye," replied the beldame, "though no witch, it is easy for me to tell you what you are about to find. Say the word you were bid repeat here, and I will conduct you where you desire to go."

"Lucca."

"Enough; follow me. He of whom you wot, will be glad that you come alone."

She led him out of the high road, by numberless lanes through which his horse could hardly break his way, among the entangled bushes of the hedges. The woman trudged on before, spinning as she went, and screaming out a few notes of a song, returning to them again and again with a monotonous kind of yell, as loud as it was discordant. At length they arrived at a mean suburb of Cremona; and, traversing a number of dirty alleys and dark streets, they came to one bounded on one side by the high, black, stone wall of a palace. The old woman knocked at a small, low door in this wall, made strong with iron clamps, and which, when cautiously opened, appeared not less in thickness than the wall of the palace itself. It was Pepi's muscular, but withered hand, that turned the massy key, and forced back the bolts of three successive doors that guarded this entrance. After having admitted Castruccio (the old woman being left behind with the horse, to lead him to the front gate of the palace), he closed the doors with care; and then, it being quite dark within the passage, he uncovered a small lamp, and led the way through the gallery, up a narrow staircase, which opened by a secret door on the great and dreary hall of the palace. This vast apartment was hardly light, although at the further end a torch, stuck against the wall, flared with a black and smoky flame.

"Welcome again, noble Castruccio, to my palace," said Pepi: "I have waited anxiously for your arrival, for all my hopes appear now to depend upon you. At present, since you appear wet and cold, come to the further hall, where we shall find fire and food: and pardon, I intreat you, my homely fare, for it is by œconomy and privation that I have become that which I am."

The manners of Pepi were unusually inflated and triumphant; and Castruccio wondered what new scene a being, whom he considered as half a buffoon, and half a madman, intended to act. A large fire blazed in the middle of the second hall, and a pot hung over it containing the supper of the family: Pepi took Castruccio's cloak, and spread it carefully on the high back of a chair; and then he pushed a low bench close to the fire, and the two friends (if so they might be called) sat down. There was no torch or lamp in the room; but the flame of the burning wood cast a broad glare on Benedetto's face, which Castruccio observed with curiosity; his brows were elevated, his sharp eyes almost emitted sparks of fire, his mouth was drawn down and compressed with a mixed expression of cunning and pride; he threw another log on the blazing hearth, and then began to speak:—

"My lord Castruccio, I think it were well that we should instantly enter on our business, since, when we have agreed upon our terms, no time must be lost in our proceeding. My proposition last May, was, as you may remember, to restore this town to the Ghibelines; and this is in my power. Cane, the lord of Verona, is I know about to approach with an army to besiege it, and it rests with me whether he shall succeed or not. If he do not agree to my terms, he must fail, as I may well say that the keys of this town rest with me. It is true, that when I spoke to you in May, I did not know that Can' Grande would attempt the town, and in that case I should have needed no more aid from you than your mere interposition: but in affairs of importance a mediator's is not a humble task; and I hope that you will not disdain to act a friendly part towards me."

Pepi paused with an inquisitive look; and Castruccio, assuring him of his amicable dispositions, intreated him to continue his explanation, and to name what he called his terms. Benedetto continued: "My terms are these, and truly they may easily be fulfilled; of course Cane only wishes to take the town out of the hands of the Guelphs, and to place it in trust with some sure Ghibeline; now let him make me lord of Cremona, and I will engage, first to put the town into his hands, and afterwards on receiving the investiture, to aid him with men during war, and pay him a tribute in time of peace. If he agree to this, let him only lead his troops to the gate of the town, and it shall be his without costing him one drop of blood."

Castruccio listened with uncontrolable astonishment. He looked at the wrinkled and hardly human face of the speaker, his uncouth gait and manners, and could scarcely restrain his contempt; he remembered Pepi's want of every principle and his boasted cruelty; and disgust overcame every other feeling; but, considering that it was as well to understand the whole of the man's drift, after a moment's pause he replied: "And where are the keys of the town which you say are in your possession?"

"Would you see them?" cried Pepi, starting up with a grin of triumph; "follow me, and you shall behold them."

He called his old woman, and, taking the lamp from her hand, he bade her prepare the supper; and then with quick steps he conducted Castruccio from the apartment: they crossed the court into the second hall, and he opened the door of the secret staircase. After Pepi had again carefully closed it, he opened another door on the staircase, which Castruccio had not before observed, and which was indeed entirely concealed in the dirty plaster of the wall. "Even she," said Pepi, pointing towards the hall, "even my old witch, does not know of this opening."

After closing it, he led the way through a dark gallery, to another long and narrow flight of stairs, which seemed to lead to the vaults underneath the castle. Castruccio paused before he began to descend, so deeply was he impressed with the villainy of his companion; but, remembering that they were man to man, and that he was young and strong, and his companion old and weak, and that he was armed with a sword, while Pepi had not even a knife at his girdle, he followed his conductor down the stairs. Flight after flight succeeded, until he thought they would never end; at length they came to another long gallery, windowless and damp, which by its close air indicated that it was below the surface of the ground, and then to various dreary and mildewed vaults in one of which stood two large chests.

"There," cried Pepi, "are the keys of the town."

"Where?" asked Castruccio, impatiently, "I see them not."

Pepi turned to him with a grin of joy; and, taking two keys from his bosom, he knelt down, and exerting his strength, turned them in their locks, and threw back the lids of the chests, first one, and then the other: they were filled with parchments.

"I do not understand this mummery; how can these musty parchments be the keys of your town?"

Pepi rubbed his hands with triumphant glee; he almost capered with delight; unable to stand still, he walked up and down the vault, crying, "They are not musty! they are parchments of this age! they are signed, they are sealed;— read them! read them!"

Castruccio took up one, and found it to be a bond obliging the signer to pay the sum of twenty thousand crowns on a certain day, in return for certain monies lent, or to forfeit the sum of thirty thousand, secured on the lands of a noble count of Cremona.

"They are usurious bonds," said Castruccio, throwing it down angrily.

"They are," replied Pepi, picking up the deed, and folding it carefully; "said I not well that I had the keys of the town? Every noble owes me a part, many the best part, of his estate. Many bonds are forfeited; and the mulct hangs over the signer by a single thread. There is count Grimaldi, whose bond was due the very day after his castle was plundered and burned, and his lands laid waste by the Germans; he owes me more than he can ever pay, though his last acre with his patent of nobility went with it, and he after with his brats, to beg at the doors of the Guelphs, his friends. There is the marquess Malvoglio who bought the life of his only son, a rank traitor, from the emperor by the sums which I lent him, which have never been repaid. This box is full of the bonds made before the siege of Cremona; it was concealed above in my tower when you last visited me; and this is full of those made since that time; you see the harvest the good emperor brought me. When the Germans quitted the town, my halls were filled with the beggarly Guelph nobility—'Messer Benedetto, my wife has not a garment to cover her! Messer Benedetto, my palace is in ruins! Messer Benedetto, my beds are destroyed, my walls are bare of furniture!'—'Oh! Messer Benedetto, without your aid my children must starve!'

"'Aye, my friends,' said I, 'I will help you most willingly; here are parchments to sign, and gold to spend!—For in the interim I had called in my debts from various other towns, and had two chests of gold ready for the gaping hounds; some read the bonds, and complained of the conditions; the greater number signed without reading them; none have been paid; now they are all mine, body and soul; aye, with these bonds, the devil himself might buy them."

"And this is the trade by which you have become rich, and to support which you have sold your paternal estate?"

"Ah! Messer Castruccio," replied Pepi, his countenance falling; "not only have I sold every acre, but I have starved myself, exposed myself by my beggarly garb to the jeers and mocks of every buffoon and idiot, who had been weaned but a year from his mother's milk: a knight in sheep-skin was an irresistible subject for ridicule; I have been patient and humble, and by my submissive mien have lulled my debtors into security, till the day of payment passed; then I have come upon them, received no payment, but got fresh bonds, and then with renewed hypocrisy, blinded them again till I have drawn their very souls from their bodies;—and they and theirs are mine. Why, Cane is himself my debtor, here is his bond for ten thousand florins of gold, which I will burn with my own hands, when by his exertions I am made lord of Cremona."

Castruccio, who had steadily curbed his contempt, now, overcome by indignation, burst forth like thunder on his host: "Thou vile Jew," he exclaimed, "utter not those words again! Thou, lord of Cremona! A usurer, a bloodsucker!—Why all the moisture squeezed from thy miserable carcase would not buy one drop of the noble heart's tide of your debtors.—And these parchments! Thinkest thou men are formed of straw to be bound with paper chains? Have they not arms? have they not swords? Tremble, foolish wretch! Be what thou art,—a sycophant.—No, thou art not human; but in these filthy vaults thou hast swollen, as a vile toad or rank mushroom; and then, because thou canst poison men, thou wouldst lord it over them! Now, thou base-minded fellow, be advised to cast off these presumptuous thoughts, or with my armed heel I will crush thee in the dust!"

Pepi was pale with rage; and, with a malignant, distorted smile, which his quivering lips could hardly frame, he said, "Fair words, my lord of Lucca; remember this is my palace, these vaults are mine, and of these passages I alone have the key, know alone of their existence."

"Slave! do you threaten?"

Castruccio had scarcely uttered these words, when he perceived Pepi gliding behind him; with eyes that flashed fire, he darted round, and transfixed by their gaze the wretched traitor; as he cast up his arm with the passionate gesture of indignation and command, Pepi grew pale with terror; it seemed to him, as if he already felt the menaced vengance of his youthful enemy; his sharp eyes became glazed, his knees trembled, his joints relaxed, and the dagger that he had already drawn from his bosom fell from his nerveless hand. All had passed so silently, that the fall of the weapon seemed to strike like thunder on the pavement, and it re-echoed along the vaults. Castruccio smiled with a feeling too lofty even to admit contempt; it was the smile of power alone.—Pepi fell upon his knees; when, suddenly perceiving that Castruccio glanced his eye from the lamp to the parchments, and then to the lamp again, the fear of losing his precious documents overcame every other feeling, and he tried, prostrate as he was, to dart past his foe, and blow out the light; Castruccio waved his hand to keep him off and the miserable traitor again shrunk back, and fell upon the ground in an agony of impotent rage and terror.

Castruccio now spoke in a restrained and firm tone: "Fear not; I came hither as a friend; and, though you have broken your faith with me, yet will I not mine with you:—I promised not to betray your secret, and I will not. But remember; if by these or any other means you attempt to oppress your townsmen, I will raise such a nest of hornets about you, that then, as now, you may intreat my mercy. Now give me the keys of your vaults and passages; and then up, and shew me the way from this infernal den."

Trembling and aghast, his strait lips white with fear, Pepi gathered himself from the pavement; with unwilling hand he gave up the keys of his vault, cast one lingering glance on his treasure, and then, followed by Castruccio, who held the lamp, he quitted his den with a hesitating and unequal gait; for his late terror made him halt, and even his coward fear lest Castruccio should yet stab him in the back as they ascended the stairs. The doors were unlocked and thrown open; for no time was allowed, as in descending, for the careful drawing of bolts and turning of locks in their progress. Castruccio was eager to leave the pestilential air of the place, and to bid farewell to his treacherous and loathsome host. They at length arrived at the head of the staircase; and Pepi would have opened the door that led to the hall.

"Down, villain!" cried Castruccio, "let me go the shortest way from your devilish abode."

"But your cloak; you left your cloak in the further hall."

"It is my legacy to thee, old fox;—it will serve to wrap your crazed limbs, and to remind you of my promises when you descend again to your tomb."

Pepi went down stairs, and opened the several doors of his palace; and Castruccio hastened past him, feeling new life as he breathed the fresh air of the open street. His enemy, now seeing him on the other side of the gates, threw off his terrors, and collecting all his malice from his heart to his miserable physiognomy, he said: "My lord Castruccio, might I say one word to you?"

"No, not one syllable: remember this night, and so farewel."

"Yet not farewell without my curse; and that I will spit after thee, if thou hadst the speed of an eagle."

The impotent wretch grinned and stamped with rage, when he saw his enemy pass on unheeding, and quickly disappear. Yet anger was not a passion that could long hold possession of the heart of Benedetto; he remembered that his dear chests were safe; and, although he still shuddered at their imminent peril, yet he satisfied himself with the deep contempt he felt towards his foe, who had allowed him, while thus in his power, to escape unhurt.

As he ascended the stairs he gazed on the lamp, and with a ghastly smile, said: "Thou wert the instrument he purposed to use, and I will tread thee to dust. His time will come, and his heart's blood and his soul's agony shall repay me for my wrongs; and so will I wind my snares, that he himself shall proclaim me lord of Cremona."

In a journey that Castruccio made to Lombardy some years after, he enquired concerning his old enemy; and, hearing that he was dead, he listened with curiosity to the relation of the last scenes of Benedetto's life. Ten days after their interview (in the September of the year 1317), Cane della Scala approached Cremona to besiege it; but, after passing some weeks before the walls, the rains, and the ravages which had been effected in the territory of his allies, the Modenese, obliged him to withdraw. Whether Pepi were terrified by the warning of Castruccio, or feared a similar reception to his propositions from Can' Grande, cannot be known: but it is certain that he made no effort to enter into a treaty with him at that time.

In the month of March of the following year Cane received a visit from the ambitious usurer at his palace in Verona. Pepi had grown wise by experience, and in this interview managed his treaty with great skill. He bought for the occasion a vest of scarlet silk and boots of Tartarian fur; fastening on his gilt spurs, throwing his gold fringed cloak over his shoulders, and putting on his head a conical cap of the newest fashion, encircled with a golden band, he mounted a good horse; and, thus caparisoned, he appeared, in his own and in his old woman's eyes, as accomplished and noble a knight as by the stroke of a sword it were possible to dub; nor did he, in his conference with Cane, mention what his means were by which he intended to betray the city, but merely boasted of his power of admitting the army of the lord of Verona, if it should appear before the gates, and named, as the condition of this service, his being instituted its lord in vassalage to Cane, if his Ghibeline townsmen should agree to receive him as their chief. The veteran commander easily acceded to these stipulations; and, the time and other circumstances being agreed upon, Pepi returned to Cremona to prepare for his future government.

His great art consisted in attacking all the nobles for their debts at the same time; and these were so numerous, and of so considerable an amount, that it created much confusion in a town which had been enfeebled by perpetual wars. The nobles, as Castruccio had predicted, reflected that they had arms in their hands, and that their debts being all due to one man, they could by his death easily free their shoulders from a heavy burthen. It was then that Pepi began to disclose to each separately his readiness to destroy their bonds, if through their means he was admitted to be lord of Cremona. The Ghibelines objected the strong opposition they should meet with from the Guelphs; to these he confided the hopes he entertained of aid from Cane della Scala. The Guelphs, now much enfeebled, appeared more tractable, since he endeavoured to persuade them that it would be wholly in his power to prevent the Ghibelines from exiling them; and he promised to act as a moderator between the parties. He was listened to, and many promised him their assistance, each in his heart despising the usurer, but believing that each by his single vote would be of no service to raise him to the sovereignty, and that by fair words they should discharge their heavy debts.

Pepi had so managed, that he had got the keys of one of the gates into possession; he admitted the troops of the lord of Verona; but he found that after all he did not possess the influence he had hoped over the minds of his townsmen. When the Ghibeline war-cry was raised, all the Guelphs of the city, distrusting either the promises or the power of their creditor, assembled in arms; and a tumult ensued, which ended in the defeat of the popular party, and the triumphant entrance of Cane into the town.

Pepi fell in that tumult: whether by a chance-blow, or by the resolved dagger of one of his debtors, cannot be ascertained. But his dead body was discovered among the slain; and, so great was the enmity of his townsmen against him, that, although Cane and his troops had already entered the city, the whole population rushed in fury towards his palace, and in a few hours the massy walls, the high tower, and all the boasted possessions of Pepi were, as himself, a loathsome and useless ruin. The hidden and unknown vaults were undisturbed; and the paper wealth of the usurer lay buried there, to rot in peace among the mildews and damps of those miserable dungeons.

CHAPTER VI

Galeazzo Visconti at Florence.—Castruccio and Euthanasia meet at Valperga: Doubts and Reserve.

Immediately after the restoration of the marquess of Este to the government of Ferrara, Galeazzo Visconti returned to Milan; and thence, after a short delay, he made a journey to Florence. The apparent motive of this visit was to accompany a younger brother, who had been long betrothed to a Florentine lady; and the period had now arrived for the celebration of their marriage. But he had other secret views: he had heard of the engagement of Castruccio to the countess of Valperga; and, this name being famous as belonging to a Guelph family, he thought that he had now discovered the cause of the peace concluded by Castruccio with Florence, and he resolved to ascertain the motives and plans of his friend; and if the countess were really the jealous Guelph fame gave her out to be, he determined to spare neither artifice nor falsehood to disturb their union.

The destined bride of young Azzo Visconti was a near relation of Euthanasia. The family of Adimari to which she belonged, although originally Guelphs, had been united to the party of the *Bianchi*, and had been expelled with them; with the exception of that branch which adhered to the *Neri*, of which the father of Euthanasia was the chief. But the children of several of these exiles continued with those of their relations who remained in Florence; and Fiammetta dei Adimari, although the daughter of an exile of the faction of the *Bianchi*, had continued to reside in Florence under the protection of an aunt. Her father had made himself famous in the wars of Lombardy; and it was there that the union between her and Azzo Visconti had been projected.

When the youth came with Galeazzo to celebrate the marriage, Fiammetta removed to the palace of Euthanasia, it being from her abode, as the head of the family, that the bride ought to be taken, when her husband should come to demand her. Galeazzo calculated on the frequent occasions of meeting that this circumstance would afford, to commence the plot he had formed on the mind of Euthanasia.

These illustrious visitors were received with honours by the magistrates of Florence: a palace was assigned for their abode, and several nobles were commissioned to shew them all that was curious in the city. Florence was then one of the finest towns in Italy; yet certainly its beauty must have been far inferior to that which it boasts at present. Its chief ornaments were palaces of massy stone, surmounted by high towers, each able to sustain a siege: some specimens of this architecture, the Palazzo Strozzi, and the Palazzo Pitti, now a ducal residence, exist to this day. They are grand and imposing; but the sombre air which they give to the streets, was better suited to those warlike and manly times, than to the taste of the present age, when the Italian heaven shines on few who would defend their own home, though its strength were that of an impregnable fortress. The Cathedral, or Duomo, afterwards the pride of Florence, was then just commenced; but the extent of its area, and the solidity of its foundations, justified the high tone of the public decree for its erection, which declared that it should surpass in beauty every other building then existing in Italy, and be the wonder of the modern world. Among other curiosities, Galeazzo was conducted to the dens of the numerous lions and lionesses kept at the expence of the republic: there were nearly an hundred of these animals, that lived sumptuously, maintained by the superstition of the Florentines, who believed their welfare to be symbolical of that of the state.

In their visits to these wonders of Florence the Visconti were accompanied by many of the young nobles of both sexes, and Euthanasia and Fiammetta were among the number. Galeazzo, from the moment of his arrival, had directed his entire attention to the unravelling the character of Euthanasia, and from all that he heard and saw, became convinced that she was the cause of the fluctuations of Castruccio's mind, and that their union must be prevented; otherwise he would never proceed against the Guelphs with the vigorous hostility which was necessary to their suppression. At first Galeazzo kept apart from Euthanasia; he was unwilling to enter into conversation with her, until, finding out the secret chords of her mind, he might play upon them with a master's hand.

They visited among the other curiosities of Florence the tomb of the family of the Soldanieri. This vast receptacle for the dead was built under ground, and received but small light from a grated window which opened into one of the cloisters of the church: it was the custom of this family to coffin their dead in brazen statues, apparently armed *cap-à-pié*; and these statues were mounted on brazen figures of horses, so that the population of the cemetery resembled a party of armed knights ready for action. The tomb was viewed by the light of innumerable torches; and there was a grim solemnity in the appearance of this troop of bronze horses, each carrying the brazen statue which imitated the living form and mien of the corpse therein coffined, that might well strike the spectator with awe; each voice was hushed as they gazed, and the younger part of the assembly hastened to quit a place which damped all their hilarity. The lights disappeared with them; and for a while Euthanasia lingered behind almost in the dark; for the solitary torch that remained, could hardly do more than make darkness visible; and the sunbeam which had strayed from its right path into the abode of the dead, tinged with its light a few of the casques of the knights, who, though their eyes and brain were within the case, neither saw nor felt the ray. Such a sight must have impressed any one with melancholy; all was still;—Euthanasia, apparently surrounded by an armed band on horseback, for the twilight gave life to the figures, yet felt about her the silence of death; her own step, her own breath, were noisy intruders in the cavern:—nor did her mute companions rest in an enchanted sleep—they were dead,—decay was at work among their frames, and the chill of mortality exhaling from the brass, made the vault as cold as it was silent.

She left the tomb with slow steps; and, at the foot of the stairs by which she would mount to daylight, Galeazzo was waiting to conduct her. Her companions were already far distant; their voices even had died away; and, as she traversed the cloisters, she appeared little inclined to break the silence between herself and her companion. At length Galeazzo spoke; and, after a few trivial remarks on the scene which they had visited, he said:

"I have long sought the opportunity now afforded me, Madonna Euthanasia, to introduce myself more particularly to your notice. As the friend of Castruccio, I hope to find myself already recommended to some portion of your kindness and regard."

Euthanasia replied with courtesy to this speech; and Galeazzo continued: "Being at the head of the Ghibelines of Lombardy, it is not wonderful that an intimacy should subsist between Castruccio and myself;—for our interests are the same; and, if by his alliance I hope to extend my dominion in the north of Italy, I trust that my name as his friend and ally, will aid him in his future designs even on this town itself."

"His designs on this town!" repeated Euthanasia.

"Aye; for in truth he encourages the hope, whether it be wild or practicable I hardly know, of overthrowing this nest of republicans, and making himself prince or imperial vicar of Tuscany. But why should I talk of his plans to you, Madonna, who must know them far better than I? Besides, it may be dangerous to speak here, even in whispers, of such things; who knows if some Guelph may not overhear me?"

"Indeed, my lord," replied Euthanasia, with a faint smile, "you divine like an astrologer; for truly I overhear you, and I am a Guelph."

"A Guelph!" repeated Galeazzo, with well feigned astonishment;—"Are you not an Adimari? Madonna Euthanasia dei Adimari?"

"I am also countess of Valperga; and that name will perhaps unravel the enigma. Yes, my lord, I am a Guelph and a Florentine; it cannot therefore be pleasing to me, to hear that Castruccio has formed such designs upon my native town. Yet I thought that I knew him well; and, if you had not seen him since our separation, I should believe that your information was founded on some mistake. As it is—tell me, if you be not bound to secrecy, what you know of his plans."

"Madonna, Castruccio honours me with the title of his friend, and secresy and faith are the bonds of friendship. When I spoke so unguardedly of his designs, I thought I spoke to one who knew them far better than myself: if I have unawares betrayed the concealed counsels of Antelminelli, I do most bitterly repent me; and do you graciously remit to me my fault, by laying no stress on my foolish words."

Euthanasia was silent; her mind was too much disturbed to know immediately what part to take. She had believed in Castruccio's promises of peace; and the foundations of her very life seemed to give way, when his faith appeared tainted with falsehood. She knew him to be ambitious; and suddenly the thought struck her, that Galeazzo alluded only to his romantic conception of future union among the Italian states, into which she also had entered, and which might easily be mistaken for schemes of war and conquest. Upon this belief she renewed the conversation, and told her companion that he must have mistaken the meaning of Castruccio; that it was that chief's wish, as it was of all patriotic Italians, to unite the factions that caused so much bloodshed and misery to their country; but that war was not the measure he intended to adopt to bring about a pacific termination.

It was now Galeazzo's turn to be silent; he looked down, and answered in monosyllables, and seemed to wish to make Euthanasia believe, that she might have divined well the plans of Castruccio, though he could not himself believe they were of so peaceful a nature. Euthanasia continued to talk; for she seemed to gather faith in what she desired from her own words. Galeazzo remained silent, and replied with downcast eyes to her appealing words and looks;—at length, after a pause, he appeared to make a struggle to throw off the embarassment of his demeanour; and looking up, "Madonna," said he, "let me intreat you to mention this subject no more. If I thought that your conjectures were right, I would frankly say so; but I do not;—each word that you utter makes me believe that Antelminelli conceals his true designs from you; and, since he has chosen me as the depositary of his secret, I should be a traitor to friendship and honour, if I disclosed it. You will see him soon, and then you can unravel the mystery; in the mean time, I pray you rest content with my assurance, that Castruccio meditates nothing unworthy his name and glory."

These few words destroyed the peace of Euthanasia. She became sorrowful and disturbed; her countenance, betraying the secret of her heart, no longer displayed that calm and softness which were before its characteristics; the brightness of her eyes, if it was not quenched, only shone forth at intervals, and she mingled most unwillingly in the festivities of the nuptial ceremony.

Galeazzo watched her carefully; he perceived the effect his words had had on her; and he determined to follow them up by a system of conduct, which should leave no doubt in her mind as to the truth of his assertions. Instead of avoiding Euthanasia, he now sought her society on all occasions, and often talked to her of Castruccio, whom he always mentioned in a style of excessive praise; yet with this he contrived to mix words, hints, or looks, which seemed to say that he followed other counsels, and devised other schemes than those of which she was aware; meanwhile all this was done in so light a manner, touched on so cursorily, and then dismissed, that, as she listened, the clue of truth slipt from her, and she felt as if lost in a pathless wilderness.

The preparations for the marriage were sumptuous. Every day large parties assembled at the palace of Euthanasia; and, when the day declined, song and dance passed away the hours of darkness. The day at length arrived, when Fiammetta should first be led to church, and thence to the palace where her husband resided. Early in the morning she and her noble friends of her own sex prepared for the ceremony, by attiring themselves in the most magnificent manner. Gold and jewels sparkled on their robes, and their dark hair twisted with pearls, hung in tresses on their shoulders; married ladies only were admitted to the nuptial procession and feasts; and Euthanasia alone, as an independent chieftainess and sovereign, claimed an exemption from this rule.

This day, so gay in appearance, and full of joyous demonstrations, Euthanasia had passed more sadly, than if she had spent it in silence and solitude, where she would not have been obliged to hide the sorrow she felt at her heart. In the evening Galeazzo informed her, that a courier, coming from Ferrara, had brought a letter to him from Castruccio; and he appeared with difficulty to yield to her intreaties to shew it to her. It contained merely excuses for his delay at Ferrara, and mentioned his speedy return:—"Yet," added he, "I shall not meet you in the cave of the Lioness[6], for you will surely be gone before my return. Were it not for a pearl which the wild animal guards for me, I would never enter her den but as her enchainer. But no more of this: you know my plans; and, if the viper and the eagle unite in firm accord, surely both her heel and her head may receive a deadly wound."

The meaning of these words was too plain; the viper was the crest of the Visconti, the eagle of the Antelminelli, and union between them was to destroy fair Florence, her native city. Euthanasia felt sick at heart; she gave back the letter in silence, and looked as a lily bent by the wind, which bows itself in patience and suffering to the storm. She remembered her vow not to unite herself to the enemy of Florence; and she resolved to abide by it. Her residence of these few weeks in her native town had endeared its inhabitants to her; she had renewed her early friendships; she was again among them, one of them;—and could she unite herself to a man who would bring havoc upon her best friends? She dreaded the reproachful voice of her conscience; and, in her well regulated mind, the fear of self-condemnation would have been sufficient to deter her from incurring such a penalty: but all the feelings of her heart here interposed; her youthful friendships; her daily habits of intercourse and mutual kindness. The favourite companion of her younger days was now married to the chief of one the citizen-bands of Florence, who would be exposed foremost to the swords of Castruccio's soldiers; the dearest friend of her father would lead his troop also against them. Her marriage with him, on condition of being a party in his victories over the Florentines, and rejoicing in the death of those she loved, would be as if she united herself to the rack, and bound herself for life, body and soul, to the ever renewing pangs of some tyrant-invented torture. It could not be: her resolution was made; and the energy of her soul qualified her to complete the sacrifice.

The following day Galeazzo and his brother returned with Fiammetta to Milan. They took a kind leave of Euthanasia; and the last words of Galeazzo were, "Forget, Madonna, all that I may have said to pain you; let not Castruccio find that I have done him an ill office in your favour; and be assured that my sorrow will be most poignant, if you find that I have infused *erroneous* ideas into your mind as to his plans and wishes."

Shortly after their departure, news arrived that Castruccio would return to Florence in two days. Euthanasia heard this with trembling;—but a short time before she had earnestly desired to see him, that she might clear up all her suspicions, and that certainty of good or evil might decide her fate;— now she feared the death that might suddenly come to all her hopes; and she felt as if but to gain a day, or a few hours, of doubt and expectation, were to gain so much of life: to insure this she took the hasty resolution of quitting Florence, and returning to her castle before the arrival of her suitor. Accordingly, attended by her domestics alone, after having taken a sudden leave of her friends, she departed.

How different was her present journey from that undertaken with Castruccio but a few months before! She was then happy and confiding; but now anxious doubt pervaded her, and fears that would not sleep. She had resolved, if the ambition of Castruccio could not content itself except with the destruction of the liberties of Florence, that she would never be his; but this resolution gave her no calm; the seal neither of life nor death was placed on her hopes: and she strove to expect good; while the fear of evil flushed her cheek, and filled her eyes with unshed tears. The year was on its decline; the myrtle flowers had faded from the mountains, and the chesnut-woods were tinged with brown and yellow; the peasants were busy among the vines; and the trellised arbours they had formed, and the sweet shades of green among which the purple grapes hung, were now pulled down, defaced and trodden upon: the swallows were collecting for their flight, and the chill mornings and evenings announced the near approach of hoary winter. The sluggish scirocco blotted the sky with clouds, and weighed upon the spirits, making them dull and heavy as itself.

Euthanasia saw all this with the observant eye of grief, which refers all things to itself, and forms omens for its own immortality from combinations more unsubstantial than the Sybilline leaves. The autumnal rains threatened nigh at hand; and the year had been much curtailed of those sweet days which follow the hot Italian summer, when the hunter feels his bow injured by the heavy dews of night, but when the noonday sun shines with tempered heat, and sets leaving the downcast eyelids of night heavy with tears for his departure; when we feel that summer is gone, and winter is coming, but the fresh-looking evergreens, the stately cypress, the fruit-burthened olive, and the dark ilex, tell us that nature is not merely a fair-weather friend. Our sorrowing traveller compared the quick advance of winter that she now witnessed, with its long delay of the preceding year, and sighed.

She arrived at her castle on the first of October; and the moment she had arrived, the storm, which for many days had been collecting from the south the force of autumnal rains and thunders, broke over her head. The white lightning sped in forked chains around the sky, and without pause or interval, deluged the midnight heaven with light, which shewed to her, as she stood at the window of her apartment, the colours of the trees, and even of the few flowers which had survived to witness the advent of the storm. The thunder broke in tremendous and continued peals, and the rain awoke in a moment the dried up sources of the mountain torrents; yet their liquid career was not heard amidst the tumult: for, if the thunder paused, the echoes prolonged the sound, and all nature seemed labouring with the commotion. Euthanasia watched the progress of the tempest; and her ear, filled with its almost deafening noise, could not distinguish the sounds, which at other times would have been audible, of horses' hoofs as they ascended the rock of Valperga, or the clang at the castle-gate, or the letting down of the draw-bridge; the first sound alien to the storm that visited her sense, was her own name pronounced in a well known and soft voice:

"Euthanasia!"

"Castruccio! you here?"

"Yes, it is I,—Castruccio;—yet I will instantly depart, if you command. I have followed fast upon your steps;—but why are you here? Why did you not remain at Florence?"

For nearly two years Euthanasia had cherished, unblamed by herself, the most fervent love for Castruccio. The union had been delayed; but the sentiment continued as a deep and clear stream, or rather like a pure lake, which in its calmness reflects more vividly and enduringly the rock that hangs eternally above it, than does the tempest-shaken water. They had been separated nearly three months; and, now that she saw and heard him again, her first impulse was, clasped in his arms, to seal with one caress a joyous forgiveness; but she checked herself. Confounded by his sudden appearance, and distracted by the many feelings that pressed upon her, she wept:—she wept long and silently; while her lover stood near her without speaking, looking at her by the glare of the continued lightnings, as they flashed in fast succesion, and made day in the chamber.

After a long pause, he spoke with less impetuosity: "Why did you not remain at Florence?"

She looked up at him, and her voice quivered, as she replied: "I cannot tell you now; I am confused, and words refuse themselves to me: my heart is full, and I am most unhappy,—to-morrow I will explain all."

"Now or never;—Euthanasia, you must not trifle with me,—are you mine?"

"If you are your own."

"What does this mean?" cried Castruccio, starting. "Of what then do you accuse me? You speak in riddles: understand, I intreat you, a plain speech, and answer me with frankness. I love you; I have long loved you; and you alone have so long delayed the union which God knows how much I desire. Now you have brought it to a crisis:—Will you be mine?"

It is difficult to answer the language of passion with that of reason: besides Euthanasia was not herself passionless, and there was a feeling in her heart that pleaded more strongly in Castruccio's favour than all his arguments. She felt subdued; yet she was angry with herself for this, and remained a long time silent, endeavouring to collect herself. At length she replied:

"Why do you press me to answer you now? or rather, consult your own heart, and that will answer for me. You have known mine long.—I love you;—but I have other duties besides those which I owe to you, and those shall be fulfilled. My father's lessons must not be forgotten, when the first occasion arrives for putting them in practice; nor must I be wanting to that sense of duty, which until now has been the rule of my life. I am a Florentine; Florence is my native country; nor will I be a traitor to it."

"Well,—and what do you conclude from this?"

"Are you not the enemy of Florence? Are you not contriving war and chains for its happy and free state? You turn away impatiently; to-morrow I will see you again, and you will then have reflected on my words: my fate depends on your true and frank reply to my question. Now leave me; I am worn out and fatigued, and to-night I cannot support the struggle into which you would lead me. To-morrow I shall see you; farewel; the storm has now passed, and the rain has quite ceased. Good night!"

"You leave me thus; and thus you reward me for suspense, jealousy and despair. Good night, Euthanasia. You sacrifice me to a bubble, to the shadow of a bubble,—be it so! Great God! that you should be influenced by such a chimæra! Well, you decide; and I shall expect your award with what patience I may. Again, good night."

He left her to doubt, suspense and grief. But her high mind bore her through all; and, having marked for herself the line of duty which she believed she ought to pursue, the natural enthusiasm of her character aided her to struggle with the misery which her sensibility inflicted upon her. Castruccio himself came to her aid; and the events which followed fast on the scene of this night, served to strengthen her resolution, and, if they did not make the sacrifice more easy, they rendered its necessity more palpable.

[6]Florence.

CHAPTER VII

Castruccio exiles three hundred Families from Lucca—Visits at Valperga—His Character further developed.

During his absence Castruccio had reduced in his own mind his various political plans to a system. He no longer varied either in the end which he desired to attain, or the means by which he resolved to accomplish it. He thought coolly on the obstacles in his way; and he resolved to remove them. His end was the conquest of Tuscany; his means, the enslaving of his native town; and, with the true disposition of a conqueror and an usurper, he began to count heads to be removed, and hands to be used, in the furtherance of his designs. He had no sooner returned to Florence, than messengers brought him intelligence of a plot, which would speedily break out in Lucca to deprive him of his government; and this information, joined to the departure of Euthanasia, determined him instantly to return to the Lucchese territory.

He was no longer the same as when he had quitted it; he returned full of thought,—with a bent brow, a cruel eye, and a heart not to be moved from its purpose by weakness or humanity. The change might appear sudden, yet it had been slow;—it is the last drop that overflows the brimming cup,—and so with him the ambition, light-heartedness, and pride which he had long been nourishing, now having made for itself a form, "a habitation and a name," first manifested itself in its true colours to the eyes of man. Ambition, and the fixed desire to rule, smothered in his mind the voice of his better reason; and the path of tyranny was smoothed, by his steady resolve to obtain the power, which under one form or other it had been the object of his life to seek.

The morning after his return to Lucca he reviewed his troops: they were devoted to him, and by their means he intended to secure his power. He assembled the senate, and surrounded the palace of government with his soldiers; he took his seat at its head, with the countenance of one who knows, and can punish his enemies. He addressed the assembly in few words, saying, that it was by their power he had been raised to the government, and that it now behoved them to support him in its exercise. "I know," he cried, "I have many enemies here,—but let any one of them step forth, and say the ill that I have done to the republic;—I who have fought its battles, secured its prosperity, and raised it from the being the servant of proud Florence to be its rival. What, will none of you come forward to denounce me, now that I appear, face to face, to answer your accusations? Randolfo Obizzi, I call upon you, who would despoil me of the power this senate conferred upon me;—

and you, Aldino, who have plotted even my death;—can ye whisper as traitors, and cannot ye speak as men? Away!—the moment of mercy is short:—three hours hence the gates of Lucca will be shut, and whoever among you or your partizans are found within its walls, will pay the forfeit of his life for his temerity."

The senate would now have broken up; but, when Castruccio saw that his enemies had all departed, he called on the rest to stay, and aid him on this momentous occasion. The decree for banishing the conspirators was then formally passed, and another for demolishing three hundred towers of so many palaces, which were as strong holds and fortresses within the town. The senate was then dismissed,—the troops paraded the streets, and before night-fall three hundred families, despoiled of their possessions, and banished their native town, passed through its gates in mournful procession. The soldiers were employed in demolishing the towers; and the ruins were carried to the eastern quarter of the city, to be used in the erection of a new wall. Castruccio, now master of Lucca, and triumphant over his enemies, felt that he had taken the first step in the accomplishment of his plans.

Euthanasia had remained in her castle in anxious expectation of a visit or a message from Castruccio;—neither came: but late in the afternoon Teresa Obizzi, one of her dearest friends, was announced to her.

"Why so mournful, dear Teresa?" asked her friend. "What has happened? Are you also unfortunate?"

"I hardly know what has happened, or where I am," replied Teresa. "Methinks the thunder of heaven has fallen among us; all the Obizzi family is banished Lucca, and not these alone, but the Bernardi, the Filippini, the Alviani, and many more, are exiled, and their possessions confiscated."

"Why, how is this? What new change has occurred in Lucca?"

"Nothing new, dear countess. In truth I believe there was a plot against Antelminelli, and that some of the Obizzi were concerned in it. But Castruccio examines nothing; and, including us all in one general sentence, has wrapt us like a whirlwind, and carries us, God alone knows whither. And my poor father! I threw myself at the consul's feet; yes, I, the wife of the proud Galeotto Obizzi, and prayed that my poor father might be allowed to remain."

"And he refused?"

"He said, 'You have heard the sentence; he best knows whether he be implicated in it; I have sworn by God and St. Martin that this nest of Guelphs and *Neri* shall be rooted out of Lucca, and that the will of the senate shall be obeyed. Let him look to it; for after three hours the life of a partizan of the Obizzi will be held no dearer than the earth on which I tread.'"

"Castruccio said this? Did he answer you thus, Teresa?"

"He did, dear Euthanasia; but I must away; I came to bid you farewel,—a long farewel; my father and my husband wait for me; pray God to pity us;—farewel!"

"Not so, Teresa. This castle is not his, and may afford an asylum to his victims. Come here; repose here awhile at least. Bring your father, your babes; come and teach me what sorrow is, and learn from me to bear it with fortitude."

As the evening advanced, others of her friends arrived, and confirmed all that Euthanasia had before heard. She was confounded, and unable to believe that it was indeed Castruccio who had caused these evils. Whence arose this sudden change in his character? Yet, was it sudden? or, was there indeed any change? She remembered words and looks, before forgotten, which told her that what now took place was the offspring of deep thought and a prepared scheme. Yet again, unable to believe the full extent of the evil that she heard, she sent to Lucca to intreat Arrigo Guinigi to hasten to her. Arrigo was with Castruccio when the message came.

"Go, my dear boy," said the latter; "her woman's heart trembles perhaps at this day's work. Shew her the necessity of it; and make her think as little unkindly of me as you can. Notwithstanding her coldness and perplexing ideas about duty, I love her, and must not have her be my enemy. If she would be content with any thing except the peace with Florence for her *morgincap*, all my power and possessions were at her feet[7]."

Arrigo went to Valperga: Euthanasia saw him alone; and, pale and almost breathless, she asked what had caused this change, and whether he knew what the schemes of Castruccio were?

"Indeed, Madonna," replied Arrigo, "I do not; I believe that he aims only at the security of his own state; and many of those he has exiled had plotted against his government."

"It is possible; tyrants ever have enemies; but it were as well to raze the city, as to banish all her citizens. There cannot be less than a thousand souls included in his edict; women and infants, torn from all the comforts, all the necessaries of daily life, cast upon the world to weep and call down curses on him. What does he mean?"

"He suspects all whom he has banished, and has strong secret reasons for his conduct; of that, Euthanasia, you may be sure. When I asked him why he banished so many of his fellow-citizens, he replied laughing, 'Because this city is not big enough for them and me.' And then he told me seriously, that his life was alone preserved by the vigorous measures of this morning."

"Be it so; I wish I could believe him; I do indeed trust that there is nothing wanton in his severity; yet methinks he had better have banished himself, than so many families, who now go as beggars through the world. He also was banished once; they say that princes learn from adversity; I believe it; they learn a cunning in cruelty the prosperous can never know."

"Nay, dear countess, speak not so hardly of him. Castruccio was born to rule; he is noble-minded, but firm of resolution; and can you blame him for securing a life on which the welfare of Lucca, perhaps of Italy, depends?"

Euthanasia did not reply; she knew, although from the gentleness of her nature she had never participated in it, that there was then in Italy a spirit of cruelty, a carelessness for the life and pain of others, which rendered it less wonderful that Castruccio should have adopted a mode of conduct similar to that of most of his contemporaries. It is strange, that man, born to suffering, and often writhing beneath it, should wantonly inflict pain on his fellows; but however cruel an individual may be, no one is so remorseless as a ruler; for he loses even within himself the idea of his own individuality, and fancies that, in pampering his inclinations, and revenging his injuries, he is supporting the state; the state, a fiction, which sacrifices that which constitutes it, to the support of its mere name. Euthanasia knew that she ought not to apply the same rule of conduct to a prince, as to a private individual; yet that Castruccio should have tainted himself with the common vices of his tribe, was a shock, that unsettled the whole frame of her mind; it unveiled at once the idol that had dwelt in the shrine of her heart, shewed the falseness of his apotheosis, and forced her to use her faculties to dislodge him from the seat he had usurped.

A few days after, Castruccio came himself to the castle of Valperga. He came at a time when many other visitors were there, and among them several whom he knew to be his secret enemies. He took no notice of this; but, with the frankness of manner for which he was remarkable, he entered into conversation with them, and treating them as on a perfect equality with himself, he soon softened the angry mood with which they had at first regarded him. All political discussion was avoided; and the conversation turned on one of those domestic tragedies which were then too common among the petty courts of Italy, where each little lord possessing supreme power, and unrestrained by principle, was ever ready to wash supposed dishonour from his name in the blood of those who had caused the stigma. The one at present under discussion was of peculiar horror, and was the more singular, since nature had vindicated her violated laws on their infringer, and he who boasted of his morality in indulging his passionate revenge, was now pursued by remorse and madness, and the ghosts of his victims hunting him through the world, gave him no rest or hope. One of the company, a Milanese, said, that it was impossible that remorse could have caused the madness of Messer Francesco; since in revenging the injury his wife had done him, he only followed the example set him by hundreds of his countrymen; and if he had gone beyond them in cruelty, it merely proved that his love, and his sense of honour transcended theirs.

Castruccio replied; "Far be it from me to plead for those childish notions, which would take the sword out of the hand of princes, and make them bind men of iron with chains of straw. But it does surprize me, that any man should dare so to idolize himself, as to sacrifice human victims at the shrine of his pride, jealousy or revenge. Francesco was a monster, when he tortured and murdered his wife; he is now a man, and feels the fitting remorse for so foul a deed. Man may force his nature, and commit deeds of horror; but we are all human beings, all the children of one common mother, who will not suffer that one should agonize the other, without suffering in his turn a part of the anguish he has inflicted[8]."

After a time the other visitors departed; and Euthanasia was left alone with Castruccio. For a while they were silent; the changeful colours of her cheek might shew, that love had not forgotten its accustomed course, but rushed in a warm flood to her heart, and then ebbed, commanded by a power hardly less strong than that which bids the ocean pause; the power of virtue in a well formed human heart. Castruccio watched her; but, in the returning calmness of her eye, and in her unhesitating voice when she did speak, he read all of female softness, but none of female weakness.

"Will you pardon me," she said, at length, "if I speak frankly to you; and not take in ill part the expression of those reflections to which your late words have given rise?"

Castruccio smiled, and replied, "Madonna, I know already what you are about to say; but you are mistaken in your conclusions. I said that no man could with impunity sacrifice the lives of his fellow-creatures to his own private passions; but you must not torture my meaning; the head of a state is no longer a private man, and he would act with shameful imbecility, if he submitted to his enemies because he dared not punish them."

Euthanasia replied to this, and drew a lively picture of the sufferings of the exiles; but Castruccio answered laughing, "You speak to one wiser on that subject than yourself. Have not I been an exile? and do you think that I forget our mournful procession, when we poor Ghibelines left Lucca nearly twenty years ago? And do you think that the *Neri* would have reigned, if they had not turned us out; and how should I reign, if I permitted this horde of Guelphs to sit here, and plot in my citadel? Their very number is an argument against them instead of being one in their favour. But let us leave this discussion, my too compassionate Euthanasia, and for a moment cast our thoughts on our own situation. There must be some end put to the riddle, some crown to a work, which seems as if it were to have no conclusion. I will be frank with you; I am neither going to turn hermit, and, laying down my sceptre, to take up with a crucifix: nor like your friends, the holy fathers of the church, am I going to war with money and falsehood, instead of with my sword. I am lord of Lucca, and shall continue so as long as God permits me. I am at the head of the Ghibelines in Tuscany, and my design is that the Ghibelines should put down their old enemies; and, seeing a fair prospect of success, I shall neither spare words nor blows against those who would oppose me in this undertaking. You are a Guelph; but surely, my dear girl, you will not sacrifice your happiness to a name, or allow party-spirit to get the better of all the more noble feelings of your nature."

Euthanasia listened with attention, and answered in mild sadness; "It does not appear to me, Castruccio, that I sacrifice any thing noble in my nature, when I refuse to unite myself to the enemy of my country. As a Ghibeline you know that I loved you; and it is not words alone that cause my change; fight the Florentines with words only, and I am still yours. But more than I love Florence, or myself, or you, Castruccio, do I love peace; and my heart bleeds to think that the cessation of bloodshed and devastation which our poor distracted country now enjoys, is to be of short duration. Have you not lived in a country suffering from war? Have you not seen the peasants driven from their happy cottages, their vines torn up, their crops destroyed, often a poor child lost, or haplessly wounded, whose every drop of blood is of more worth than the power of the Cæsars? And then to behold the tears and despair of these poor creatures, and to find men who would still inflict them,—and for what? The bubble is yours, Castruccio.—What would you have? Honour, fame, dominion? What are these if peace do not purchase them, but contempt, infamy and despotism! Oh! rule your own heart; enthrone reason there, make virtue the high priest of your divinity; let the love of your fellow-creatures be your palace to dwell in, and their praises your delicate food and costly raiment; and, as all sovereigns have dungeons, so do you have them, in which your pride, ambition, and, forgive the word, your cruelty, may be enchained; and then the purple-clad emperors of Constantinople may envy your state and power.

"Why do you cause this cruel combat? or, why would you increase the struggle in my heart? As the enemy of Florence I will never be yours; as the deliberate murderer of the playmates of my infancy, of the friends of my youth, of those to whom I am allied by every tie of relationship and hospitality that binds mankind, as such, I will never be yours. Here then is the crown of the work; the sea in which the deep and constant stream of my affections loses itself,—your ambition. Let these be the last words of contest between us: but if, instead of all that I honour and love in the world, you choose a mean desire of power and selfish aggrandizement, still listen to me. You are about to enter on a new track, yet one on which the course of thousands of those that have gone before you is to be seen: do not follow these; do not be sanguinary like them;—the Italians of the present day have all a remorseless cruelty in them, which will stain the pages of their history with the foulest blots; let yours be free from these!

"Pardon me that I speak to you in this strain. From this moment we are disjoined; whatever our portions may be, we take them separately. Such is the sentence you pronounce upon us."

Castruccio was moved by the fervour of Euthanasia; he tried to alter her determination, to argue her from the point of difference between them, but in vain; he moved her to tears. She wept, but did not reply: her purpose was fixed, but her heart was weak; she loved for the first and only time; and she knew that she sacrificed every hope and joy in life, if she sacrificed Castruccio. But she was firm, and they parted; a parting that caused every nerve in Euthanasia's frame to thrill with agony.

She tried to still these feelings, to forget that she loved; but tears, abundant tears, alone eased the agony of her heart, when she thought, that the soft dreams she had nourished for two years were vain, gossamer that the sun of reality dissipated. Sometimes she schooled herself as being too precise and over-wise, to sacrifice all her hopes to the principles she had set up. But then the remembrance of the grief she had endured during the last war with Florence, and the worse struggles she would feel, if she dared unite herself to an enemy, if, by binding her fate to his, she might neither pray for the cause of her husband, nor for that of her beloved country; when to wish well to Castruccio would be to desire the success of tyranny and usurpation; and to have given her vows to the Florentines in their necessary defence, was to wish the overthrow of the companion of her life—the idea of these struggles gave her courage to persevere; and she hoped, that the approbation of her own heart, and that of her dearest and most valued friends, would in some degree repay her for her sufferings. She thought of her father and his lessons; and her heart again swelled with the desire of the approbation of the good, with the warm and ardent love of right which ever burned within her soul. Hers had been a natural and a lawful passion; she could not live, believing that she did wrong; and the high independence and graceful pride of her nature would never permit her, to stoop beneath the mark she had assigned as the object of her emulation.

Yet when, in the silence of night and of solitude, she consulted her own heart, she found that love had quenched there every other feeling, and not to love was to her to die. She looked on the quiet earth, where the trees slept in the windless air, and the only sound was the voice of an owl, whose shriek now and then with monotonous and unpleasing sound awoke the silence, and gave a melancholy life to what else were dead; she looked up to the sky where the eternal lamps of heaven were burning; all was unchanged there; but for her all was different. It was on a night, in an Italian autumn, that she sat under her acacia tree by the basin of the fountain of the rock. To look on the hues of sunset, to see the softened tints of the olive woods, the purple tinge of the distant mountains, whose outline was softly, yet distinctly marked in the orange sky; to feel the western breeze steal across her cheek, like words of love from one most dear; to see the first star of evening penetrate from out the glowing western firmament, and whisper the secret of distant worlds to us in our narrow prison; to behold the heaven-pointing cypress with unbent spire sleep in the stirless air; these were sights and feelings which softened and exalted her thoughts; she felt as if she were a part of the great whole; she felt bound in amity to all; doubly, immeasurably loving those dear to her, feeling an humanizing charity even to the evil. A sweet scent coming from the lemon-flowers, which mingled with the gummy odour of the cypress trees, added to the enchantment. Suddenly,—list! what is that? Music was heard, and sweeter than all other instruments, the human voice in chorus singing a national song, half hymn, half warlike; Euthanasia wept; like a child she wept,—but there was none near to whom she could tell the complicated sensations that overpowered her: to speak to those we love in such moments, exhilarates the spirits; else the deep feeling preys on the heart itself. She became sad, and looked up to the many-starred sky; her soul uttered silently the bitter complaint of its own misery.

"Must I then forget to love? Oh! sooner shall that restless lamp, which walketh up the heavens, and then descendeth, and abideth no where, Oh! sooner shall that forget its path which it hath ever traced, since God first marked it out, than I forget to love! The air still surrounds the earth, filling the recesses of the mountains, and even penetrating into their caverns; the sun shines through the day, and the cloudless heavens of night are starred with the air's fire-bearing children; and am not I as unchanged and unchangeable as nature's own, everlasting works? What is it then that startles every nerve, not as the sound of thunder or of whirlwind, but as the still, small voice, that clings to me, and will not be made silent, telling me that all is changed from that which it once was?

"I loved! God and my own heart know how truly, how tenderly! How I dwelt on his idea, his image, his virtues, with unblamed affection: how it was my glory, my silent boast, when in solitude my eyes swam in tears, and my cheek glowed, to reflect that I loved him, who transcended his kind in wisdom and excellence! Is this a dream? Oh! then all is a dream; and the earth, and the fabric of the adamantine sky are as the gossamer that may not endure! Yet, oh, ye stars, ye shine! And I live. Pulse, and breath, and thought, and all is changed; I must no longer love,—so let me suffer the living death of forgetfulness.

"Surely my heart is not cold, for I feel deep agony; and yet I live. I have read of those who have pined and died, when the sweet food of love was denied to them; were their sensations quicker, deeper, more all-penetrating than mine? Their anguish greater? I know not; nor do I know, if God hath given this frame a greater capacity for endurance than I could desire. Yet, methinks, I still love, and that is why I live. A dark, blank, rayless, motionless night is before me, a heavy, overwhelming annihilation is above me, when for a moment I imagine that hope is not for me. But for an instant does that idea live within me, yet does it come oftener and stay longer that it was wont. The knowledge that I have nought to expect but death, must become a part of my mind. When a dear friend dies, what painful throes does one undergo, before we are persuaded to know that he is no more! So now that hope dies; it is a lesson hard for my heart to learn; but it will learn it; and that which is now reality, will be as a dream; what is now a part of me will be but a recollection, a shadow thrown upon life, from which I at length shall emerge. And what is the state of being that shall follow?

"Yet will I arouse all the pride and all the nobility of my nature; I will not sink beneath this trial; the great and good of past ages have left their lessons for me to meditate, and I will be no indocile pupil; the honey of the cup is exhausted, but all is not gall that remains."

The winter passed on thus: Euthanasia feared Castruccio as the enemy of *Florence*; but she avoided Florence as *his* enemy. Disappointed in her dearest hopes, her very heart destroyed, she hated society, and felt solace in the contemplation of nature alone; that solace which the mind gathers, in communing with its sorrows, and, having lost every other resource, clings as to a friend, to the feelings of woe with which it is penetrated.

The winter was chill; the mountains were covered with snow; yet, when the sun gleamed on them, the Serchio, taking life from his smiles, sped down in his course, roaring and howling, as if, pursued by innumerable and overflowing streams, he hurried to find repose in his home among the waters of the boundless ocean. The air was filled with his turmoil; and winter, asleep among the icy crags of the mountains, feared a sound, which he had not power to silence, and which was the dirge that tolled out his passing hour: the cold northern wind swept along the plain of Lucca, and moaned as a repulsed beggar about the walls of Euthanasia's castle. Within those walls, late the scene of content and joy, sat the disconsolate mistress, a prey to all those sad, and sometimes wild reveries, which utter hopelessness had made her companions. Duty, and the associations of her early youth, had breathed in her ear the terrible command to love no more; but her soul rebelled, and often she thought that, in so mad a world, duty was but a watch-word for fools, and that she might unblamed taste of the only happiness she should ever enjoy.

But, in one who had so long submitted her very thoughts to the control of conscience, such ideas found brief habitation; and her accustomed feelings returned to press her into the narrow circle, whence for her all peace was excluded. Duty, patriotism, and high religious morality, were the watch-dogs which drove her scattered thoughts, like wandering sheep, into their fold: alas! the wolf nestled in the pen itself. If for a moment her will paused, and love, breaking every bank she had carefully built up to regulate her mind's course, burst in at once, and carried away in its untameable course reason, conscience, and even memory, Castruccio himself came to repair the breach, and to restrain the current; some castle burnt, some town taken by assault, some friend or enemy remorselessly banished, filled her with shame and anger, that she should love a tyrant; a slave to his own passions, the avenger of those of others. Castruccio was ever at war; peace subsisted between him and Florence; but the siege of Genoa by the Ghibelines of Lombardy, gave him occasion to turn his arms on that side; and, his march extending from Lucca to beyond the Magra, he deluged the country in blood, and obtained that which he desired, dominion and fame.

It were curious to mark the changes that now operated in his character. Every success made him extend his views to something beyond; and every obstacle surmounted, made him still more impatient of those that presented themselves in succession. He became all in all to himself; his creed seemed to contain no article but the end and aim of his ambition; and that he swore before heaven to attain. Accustomed to see men die in battle for his cause, he became callous to blood, and felt no more whether it flowed for his security on a scaffold, or in the field of honour; and every new act of cruelty hardened his heart for those to come.

And yet all good feelings were not dead within him. An increased ardour in friendship seemed to have taken the place of innocence and general benevolence: virtue, as it were seeking to build her nest in his heart, and thrust out of her ancient one, taking up with the resting-place whose entrance still was free. Bravery and fortitude were to him habitual feelings: but, although he were kind and bounteous to his friends, so that he was loved with ardour, and served with fidelity, there was no magnanimity, and little generosity in his character. His moderate habits, abstemiousness, and contempt of luxury, often gave him the appearance of self-sacrifice; for he bestowed on others what they greatly valued, but what he himself contemned. But, when it came to the sacrifice of his own inclinations, his boundless ambition, and love of sway, then no obstacle either of nature or art could stop him; neither compassion which makes angels of men, nor love which softens the hearts of the gods themselves, had over him the slightest power,—he fixed his whole soul on the point he would attain, and he never either lost sight of it, or paused in his efforts to arrive there.

It were difficult to tell what his sensations were with regard to Euthanasia; he had loved her, tenderly, passionately; and he considered her refusal of his offers as a caprice to be surmounted. Sometimes he was deeply grieved, sometimes angry; yet he ever loved her, and believed that she would relent. Sometimes he thought of poor Beatrice, her form, beaming with beauty, and alive with the spirit of the sybil; or again, pale, struck to the heart as a poor deer in the forest, and sinking beneath the wound:—he then felt that he would give the world to assuage her sorrows. On returning through Bologna, he had sent to Ferrara, and heard that she was alive, that no change in her situation had taken place; and, satisfied with this, he sought no further. Ambition had become the ruling passion of his soul, and all bent beneath its sway, as a field of reeds before the wind: love himself had brief power in his mind; and, although this passion sometimes caused him pain, and the sickness of disappointed hope, yet this was short, and yielded to the first impulse that occurred, which hurried him along to new designs and new conquests.

Once indeed he had loved, and he had drank life and joy from the eyes of Euthanasia. His journey to Lombardy, his connexion with Beatrice, although indeed he loved her little, yet was sufficient to weaken the bonds that confined him; and love was with him, ever after, the second feeling in his heart, the servant and thrall of his ambition.

His military exploits were now bounded to the entire reduction of the territory around Lucca; Sarzana, Pontremoli, Fucecchio, Fosedenovo,—castles even beyond the Magra, Valdinera, Aquabuona, La Valle, fortified villages among the Apennines, which had hitherto been under the jurisdiction of the lords of Lombardy, now submitted to the Lucchese consul. During the winter he was for some time confined by the floods to the town of Lucca itself, where he employed himself in establishing a vigorous system of police, in discovering and punishing his enemies, and in the design and foundation of public edifices. He was beloved by the nobles of his own party, and by the common people, whose taxes he lightened, and whom he relieved in a great measure from the tyranny of their superiors; he was beloved even by the clergy, for, although an enemy to the temporal usurpations of the Popes, he valued the learning, and respected the persons of the priests. He was hated by all the rich not immediately connected with his person and faction, for they were deprived of power; despised by his followers, and watched by himself, they could find no asylum from the suspicion and severity of a tyrant who felt himself insecure on his seat of power.

[7] The *morgincap* was a boon granted by the husband to the wife the morning after the nuptials. It consisted generally of a gift of part of his possessions, sometimes of the half, often of a quarter of his property. Laws were made in some states to restrain this excessive generosity, but the custom of the *morgincap* continued a long time in Florence.

[8] The story here alluded to, is told by Bandello, and is related with that air of truth which this writer delights to give to his narrations.

CHAPTER VIII

Beatrice, disguised as a Pilgrim, visits Valperga.—Castruccio relates her Story.

Spring advanced, and the mountains looked forth from beneath the snow: the chesnuts began to assume their light and fanlike foliage; the dark ilex and cork trees which crowned the hills, threw off their burthen of snow; and the olives now in flower starred the mountain paths with their small fallen blossoms; the heath perfumed the air; the melancholy voice of the cuckoo issued from the depths of the forests; the swallows returned from their pilgrimage; and in soft moonlight evenings the nightingales answered one another from the copses; the vines with freshest green hung over the springing corn; and various flowers adorned the banks of each running stream. Euthanasia beheld the advance of summer with careless eyes: her heart was full of one thought, of one image; and all she saw, whether it were the snow-clad mountains of winter, or the green and flowery fields of spring, was referred by her to one feeling, one only remembrance. She determined to think no more of Castruccio; but every day, every moment of every day, was as a broken mirror, a multiplied reflection of his form alone.

They had often met during the winter in the palaces of the Lucchese nobles, and sometimes at her own castle; he was ever gentle and deferential to her, and sometimes endeavoured to renew the courtship that had formerly subsisted between them. Euthanasia had not strength of purpose sufficient to avoid these meetings; but each of them was as the life-blood taken from her heart, and left her in a state of despair and grief that preyed like fever upon her vitals. To see him, to hear him, and yet not to be his, was as if to make her food of poison; it might assuage the pangs of hunger, but it destroyed the principle of life. She became pale, sleepless, the shadow of what she had been; her friends perceived the change, and knew the cause; and they endeavoured to persuade her to go to Florence, or to take some journey, which might occupy her mind, and break the chain that now bound her to sorrow. She felt that she ought to comply with their suggestions; but even *her* spirit, strong and self-sustaining as it had been, sank beneath the influence of love, and she had no power to fly, though to remain were death. Tears and grief were her daily portion; yet she took it patiently, as that to which she was doomed, and hardly prayed to have the bitter cup removed.

A circumstance that occurred just at this crisis, when she seemed to stand on the sharp edge which divides life from death, saved her from destruction, and led her back to taste for a few more years the food of sorrow and disappointment which was doled out to her.

The summer solstice had passed, and Castruccio had been absent during several months, carrying his conquests along the shore beyond the Magra, while every day brought the news of some fresh success he had obtained. This was the season of pilgrimages to Monte San Pelegrino, a wild and high Apennine in the neighbourhood of Valperga. It is said, that a king of Scotland, resigning his crown to his son, and exiling himself from his country, finished his days in penitence and prayer on this mountain. In Italy every unknown pilgrim was a king or prince: but this was a strange tradition; and it would seem as if the royal penitent, disdaining the gladsome plains of Italy, sought for the image of his native country on this naked peak among the heaped masses of the Apennines.

His memory was there canonized, and many indulgences were the reward of three successive visits to his rocky tomb; every year numberless pilgrims flocked, and still continue to flock thither. Straining up the rugged paths of the mountain, careless of the burning sun, they walk on, shadowed by their broad pilgrim's hats, repeating their *pater-nosters*, and thus, by the toil of the body, buy indulgence for the soul's idleness. Many on their return visited the castle of Valperga, and partook its hospitality. One party had just withdrawn, as the *Ave Maria* sounded from the vale below; and they chaunted the evening hymn, as they wound down the steep. Euthanasia listened from her tower, and heard the last song of the sleepy cicala among the olive woods, and the buz of the numerous night insects, that filled the air with their slight but continual noise. It was the evening of a burning day; and the breeze that slightly waved the grass, and bended the ripe corn with its quick steps, was as a refreshing bath to the animals who panted under the stagnant air of the day. Amid the buzzing of the crickets and dragon flies, the agiolo's monotonous and regular cry told of clear skies and sunny weather; the flowers were bending beneath the dew, and her acacia, now in bloom, crowning its fan-like foliage with a roseate crest, sent forth a sweet scent. A few of the latest fire-flies darted here and there, with bright green light; but it was July, and their season was well nigh past. Towards the sea, on the horizon, a faint lightning shewed the over-heated state of the atmosphere, and killed by its brightness the last glories of the orange sunset; the mountains were losing their various tints in darkness; and their vast amphitheatre looked like a ponderous unformed wall, closing in Lucca, whose lights glimmered afar off.

Euthanasia was awaked from the reverie, half painful, half pleasing, that engaged her as she sat at her window; for she was too true a child of nature, not to feel her sorrows alleviated by the sight of what is beautiful in the visible world;—she was roused, I say, by her servant who told her that a female pilgrim was at the gate, and desired to see the lady of the castle. "Receive her," said Euthanasia, "and let her be led to the bath, I will see her when she is refreshed."

"She will not enter," replied the servant, "but desires earnestly, she says, to see you: she absolutely refuses to enter the castle."

Euthanasia descended to the gate; her quick light steps trod the pavement of the hall, her long golden tresses waved upon the wind, and her blue eyes seemed to have drunk in the azure of departed day, they were in colour so deep, so clear. The pilgrim stood at the door leaning on her staff, a large hat covered her head, and was pulled down over her brows, and her coarse cloak fell in undistinguishing folds round her slim form; but Euthanasia, accustomed to see the peasantry alone resort to this mountain, was struck by the small white hand that held the staff, and the delicately moulded and snowy feet which, shod in the rudest sandals, seemed little used to labour or fatigue.

"I intreat you," she said, "to come into the castle to rest yourself; the *Ave Maria* is passed, and your toils for the day are ended; you will find a bath, food and rest; will you not enter?" Euthanasia held forth her hand.

"Lady, I must not. I intreat you only to bestow your alms on a pilgrim going to Rome, but who has turned aside to perform a vow among these mountains."

"Most willingly; but I also have made a vow, which is, not to suffer a tired pilgrim to pass my gates without rest and food. Where can you go to-night? Lucca is six long miles off; you are weak and very weary: come; I ask you for alms; they are your prayers which must be told on the soft cushions of a pleasant bed amid your dreams this night. Come in; the heavy dews that fall from the clear sky after this burning day may hurt you: this is a dangerous hour in the plain; can you not be persuaded?"

Euthanasia saw quick drops fall from the flashing and black eyes of the poor pilgrim: she raised them to heaven, saying, "Thy will be done! I am now all humbleness."

As she threw up her head Euthanasia looked on her countenance; it was beautiful, but sunburnt and wild; her finely carved eyes, her lips curved in the line of beauty, her pointed and dimpled chin still beamed loveliness, and her voice was low and silver-toned. She entered the castle, but would go no further than the outer hall. The eloquence of Euthanasia was wasted; and she was obliged to order cushions and food to be brought to the hall: they then sat down; the pilgrim took off her hat, and her black and silken ringlets fell around her face; she parted them with her small fingers, and then sat downcast and silent.

Euthanasia placed fruit, sweetmeats and wine before her; "Eat," she said, "you are greatly fatigued."

The poor pilgrim tried; but her lips refused the fruit she would have tasted. She felt that she should weep; and, angry at her own weakness, she drank a little wine, which somewhat revived her; and then, sitting thus, overcome, bent and sorrowing, beside the clear loveliness of Euthanasia, these two ladies entered into conversation, soft and consoling on one part, on the other hesitating and interrupted. At first the pilgrim gazed for a moment on the golden hair and bluest eyes of Euthanasia, her heavenly smile, and clear brow; and then she said: "You are the lady of this castle? You are named Euthanasia?"

"Most true: and might I in return ask you who you are, who wander alone and unhappy? Believe me I should think myself very fortunate, if you would permit me to know your grief, and to undertake the task of consoling you. If you mourn for your faults, does not a moment of real repentance annihilate them all? Come, I will be your confessor; and impose on you the light penances of cheerfulness and hope. Do you mourn your friends? poor girl! weep not; that is a sorrow time alone can cure: but time can cure it, if with a patient heart you yield yourself to new affections and feelings of kindness. Sweet, hush the storm that agitates you: if you pray, let not your words be drops of agony, but as the morning dew of faith and hope. You are silent; you are angry that I speak; so truly do I prize the soft peace that was for years the inmate of my own heart, that I would bestow it on others with as earnest a labour, as for myself I would try to recal it to the nest from which it has fled."

"How! and are you not happy?" The eyes of the pilgrim glanced a sudden fire, that was again quenched by her downcast lids.

"I have had my share of tranquillity. For five-and-twenty years few sorrows, and those appeaseable by natural and quickly dried tears, visited me; now my cares rise thick, while, trust me, with eager endeavour, I try to dissipate them. But you are young, very young; you have quaffed the gall, and will now come to the honey of your cup. Wherefore are you bound for Rome?"

"It were a long tale to tell, lady, and one I would not willingly disclose. Yet, methinks, you should be happy; your eyes are mild, and made for peace. I thought,—I heard,—that a thousand blessed circumstances conduced to render you fortunate beyond all others."

"Circumstances change as fast as the fleeting clouds of an autumnal sky. If happiness depends upon occasion, how unstable is it! We can alone call that ours which lives in our own bosoms. Yet those feelings also are bound to mutability; and, as the priests have doubtless long since taught you, there is no joy that endures upon earth."

"How is this! He is not dead!—he must be—" The pilgrim suddenly stopped, her cheek burning with blushes.

"Who dead? What do you mean?"

"Your father, your brother, any one you love. But, lady, I will intrude no longer; the dews are fallen, and I find the air of the castle close and suffocating. I long for the free air."

"You will not sleep here?"

"I must not; do not ask me again; you pain me much; I must pursue my journey!"

The pilgrim gathered up her raven locks, and put on her hat; then, leaning on her staff, she held forth her little hand, and said in a smothered voice, so low that the tone hardly struck the air, "Your alms, lady."

Euthanasia took out gold; the pilgrim smiled sadly, saying, "My vow prevents my receiving more than three soldi; let that sum be the limit of your generous aid."

Euthanasia found something so inexplicable, reserved, and almost haughty, in the manner of her guest, that she felt checked, and ill disposed to press her often rejected services; she gave the small sum asked, saying, "You are penurious in your courtesies; this will hardly buy for me one *pater-noster*."

"It will buy the treasure of my heart in prayers for your welfare; prayers, which I once thought all powerful, may be as well worth perhaps as those of the beggar whom we fee on the road-side. Farewell!"

The pilgrim spoke earnestly and sweetly; and then drawing her cloak about her, she left the castle, winding slowly down the steep. After she had awhile departed, Euthanasia sent a servant to the nunnery of St. Ursula, which was on the road the pilgrim was to follow, with a loaded basket of fruits, wine and other food, and a message to the nuns to watch for and receive the unhappy stranger. All passed as she desired. The pilgrim entered the convent; and, after praying in the chapel, and silently partaking a frugal meal of fruit and bread, she went to rest in her lowly cell. The next morning the abbess had intended to question her, and to win her to some comfort; but, before the dawn of day, the pilgrim had left the convent; and, with slow steps and a sorrowing heart, pursued her way towards Rome.

This occurrence had greatly struck Euthanasia. She felt, that there was something uncommon in the visit of the stranger, and that, although unknown to her, there must be some link between them, which she vainly strove to discover. It happened, that, about a fortnight after, she was at the Fondi palace in Lucca, where Castruccio was in company; and she related this incident, dwelling on the beauty of the pilgrim, her graceful manners, and deep sorrow. When she described her form and countenance, Castruccio, struck by some sudden recollection, advanced towards Euthanasia, and began to question her earnestly as to the very words and looks of the stranger; then, checking himself, he drew back, and entered into conversation with another person. When however Euthanasia rose to depart, he approached, and said in a low tone: "I am afraid that I can solve the riddle of this unfortunate girl; permit me to see you alone to-morrow; I must know every thing that passed."

Euthanasia assented, and waited with impatience for the visit.

He came; and at his request she related minutely all that had happened. Castruccio listened earnestly; and, when he heard what had been her last words, he cried, "It must be she! It is the poor Beatrice!"

"Beatrice!—Who is Beatrice?"

Castruccio endeavoured to evade the question, and afterwards to answer it by the relation of a few slight circumstances; but Euthanasia, struck by his manner, questioned him so seriously, that he ended by relating the whole story. Euthanasia was deeply moved; and earnest pity succeeded to her first astonishment; astonishment for her powers and strange errors, and then compassion for her sorrows and mighty fall. Castruccio, led on by the memory of her enchantments, spoke with ardour, scarcely knowing to whom he spoke; and, when he ended, Euthanasia cried, "She must be followed, brought back, consoled; her misery is great; but there is a cure for it."

She then concerted with Castruccio the plan for tracing her steps, and inducing her to return. Messengers were sent on the road to Rome, who were promised high rewards if they succeeded in finding her; others were sent to Ferrara to learn if her friends there had any knowledge of her course. These researches occupied several weeks; but they were fruitless: the messengers from Ferrara brought word, that she had left that city early in the preceding spring in a pilgrimage to Rome, and that she had never since been heard of. The lady Marchesana, inconsolable for her departure, had since died; and the good bishop Marsilio, who had not returned from France, where he had been made a cardinal, was at too great a distance to understand the circumstances of her departure, or to act upon them. Nor were the tidings brought from Rome more satisfactory; she was traced from Lucca to Pisa, Florence, Arezzo, Perugia, Foligno, Spoletto, and even to Terni; but there all trace was lost. It appeared certain that she had never arrived in Rome; none of the priests had heard of her; every church and convent was examined; but no trace of her could be found. Every exertion was vain: it appeared as if she had sunk into the bowels of the earth.

During the period occupied by these researches, a great change had taken place in the mind of Euthanasia. Before, though her atmosphere had been torn by storms, and blackened by the heaviest clouds, her love had ever borne her on towards one point with resistless force; and it seemed as if, body and soul, she would in the end be its victim. Now the tide ebbed, and left her, as a poor wretch upon one point of rock, when the rising ocean suddenly subsides, and restores him unexpectedly to life. She had loved Castruccio; and, as is ever the case with pure and exalted minds, she had separated the object of her love from all other beings, and, investing him with a glory, he was no longer to her as one among the common herd, nor ever for a moment could she confound him and class him with his fellow men. It is this feeling that is the essence and life of love, and that, still subsisting even after esteem and sympathy had been destroyed, had caused the excessive grief in which she had been plunged. She had separated herself from the rest as his chosen one; she had been selected from the whole world for him to love, and therefore was there a mighty barrier between her and all things else; no sentiment could pass through her mind unmingled with his image, no thought that did not bear his stamp to distinguish it from all other thoughts; as the moon in heaven shines bright, because the sun illumines her with his rays, so did she proceed on her high path in serene majesty, protected through her love for him from all meaner cares or joys; her very person was sacred, since she had dedicated herself to him; but, the god undeified, the honours of the priestess fell to the dust. The story of Beatrice dissolved the charm; she looked on him now in the common light of day; the illusion and exaltation of love was dispelled for ever: and, although disappointment, and the bitterness of destroyed hope, robbed her of every sensation of enjoyment, it was no longer that mad despair, that clinging to the very sword that cut her, which before had tainted her cheek with the hues of death. Her old feelings of duty, benevolence, and friendship returned; all was not now, as before, referred to love alone; the trees, the streams, the mountains, and the stars, no longer told one never-varying tale of disappointed passion: before, they had oppressed her heart by reminding her, through every change and every form, of what she had once seen in joy; and they lay as so heavy and sad a burthen on her soul, that she would exclaim as a modern poet has since done:

Thou, thrush, that singest loud, and loud, and free,
Into yon row of willows flit,
Upon that alder sit,
Or sing another song, or choose another tree!

Roll back, sweet rill, back to thy mountain bounds,
And there for ever be thy waters chained!
For thou dost haunt the air with sounds
That cannot be sustained.

* * * *

Be any thing, sweet rill, but that which thou art now

But now these feverish emotions ceased. Sorrow sat on her downcast eye, restrained her light step, and slept in the unmoved dimples of her fair cheek; but the wildness of grief had died, the fountain of selfish tears flowed no more, and she was restored from death to life. She considered Castruccio as bound to Beatrice; bound by the deep love and anguish of the fallen prophetess, by all her virtues, even by her faults; bound by his falsehood to her who was then his betrothed, and whom he carelessly wronged, and thus proved how little capable he was of participating in her own exalted feelings. She believed that he would be far happier in the passionate and unquestioning love of this enthusiast, than with her, who had lived too long to be satisfied alone with the affection of him she loved, but required in him a conformity of tastes to those she had herself cultivated, which in Castruccio was entirely wanting. She felt half glad, half sorry, for the change she was aware had been operated in her heart; for the misery that she before endured was not without its momentary intervals, which busy love filled with dreams and hopes, that caused a wild transport, which, although it destroyed her, was still joy, still delight. But now there was no change; one steady hopeless blank was before her; the very energies of her mind were palsied; her imagination furled its wings, and the owlet, reason, was the only dweller that found sustenance and a being in her benighted soul.

CHAPTER IX

Castruccio plots the Assassination of Robert King of Naples.—Made Prince of Lucca.—Declares War against Florence.—Plot for a Revolution in Lucca defeated.—Castruccio summons Valperga.

The ambitious designs of Castruccio were each day ripening. The whole Ghibeline force in Italy was now turned to the siege of Genoa, which was defended by Robert, king of Naples, at the head of the Guelphs. Castruccio had never actually joined the besieging army. But he had taken advantage of the war, which prevented the Genoese from defending their castles on the sea-coast, to surprise many of them, and to spread his conquests far beyond the Lucchese territory; and he was ever attentive to the slightest incident that might contribute to the exaltation of the Ghibelines. He aided his Lombard friends, by annoying the enemy as much as was in his power, and did not hesitate in using the most nefarious arts to injure and destroy them. He now fully subscribed to all the articles of Pepi's political creed, and thought fraud and secret murder fair play, when it thinned the ranks of the enemy.

Robert, king of Naples, was at the head of the Guelph army at Genoa. The siege had now lasted with various fortune for two years; and every summer the king visited this city to conduct the enterprizes of the campaign. Castruccio, urged by Galeazzo Visconti, and by his own belief in the expediency of the scheme, conspired to destroy the king: a foolish plan in many ways; for a legitimate king, like a vine, never dies; and when you throw earth over the old root, a new sprout ever springs up from the parent stock.

The king of Naples had fitted out a fleet to go and attack the king of Sicily, who was a protector of the Ghibelines. Castruccio sent two desperate, but faithful fellows, to set fire to the ship in which the king himself sailed. The men got admittance on board the royal galley, which, swifter than the rest, sped on through the waves, while the rest of the fleet hung like a cloud on the far horizon. At night the smell of fire was perceived in the vessel, and a small flame issued from one of the windows: the affright and confusion were terrible, when they found that they were burning thus on the desert sea, while the other vessels were too distant to afford them aid. All hands were at work to extinguish the flames; and it was then that the hired incendiaries were perceived, as they tried to fire another part of the ship. It was found that they were provided with floats of cork, by which they hoped to preserve themselves in the water, until by some accident they might be rescued.

The fire was seen by the galley, in which the eldest son of king Robert was embarked, and which bore down to his relief. The youthful prince, in an agony of terror, lent his own hand to the oar that they might arrive more speedily. The whole crew was saved; and the criminals were reserved for torture and death.

The news of this detestable plot was spread through all Italy, nor was it much blamed. It was then that Euthanasia, the living spirit of goodness and honour, amidst the anguish that the unworthiness of Castruccio occasioned her, felt a just triumph, that she had overcome her inclinations, and was not the bride of a suborner and a murderer. Even now, remembering that it was known that she once loved Antelminelli, she was penetrated with shame, and her cheeks burned with blushes when she heard the tale. But, careless of an infamy which he shared with many of his countrymen, and sorry only that his design had not succeeded, Castruccio did not attempt to conceal the part he had taken in the plot, and loudly declared that all his enemies might expect the same measure as king Robert, while in return he permitted them to try the like arts against him.

In the mean time he prosecuted the war with redoubled vigour. In the winter of the year 1320, the Ghibelines reinforced their armies before Genoa, and called upon their allies for their utmost assistance; and Castruccio among the rest was to advance to their aid with all his forces. But the Guelphs were not idle: Florence had sent soldiers every campaign to reinforce the Genoese, and entered with spirit into all the enterprizes undertaken against the imperial party; although a wish to preserve their territory free from the horrors of war, and to repair by a long peace the injury done to their vines and olive woods, had caused them to preserve a shew of peace with Lucca.

Castruccio considered all his present successes as preliminaries only to his grand undertaking; and, having now reduced not only the territory of Lucca, but many castles and strong holds, which before had either been independent, or had paid tribute to Genoa, or to the lords of Lombardy, he planned a more vigorous system of warfare for the ensuing campaign. His first step was to increase his security and power in Lucca itself.

Having grown proud upon his recent successes, he began to disdain the name of consul, which he had hitherto borne. He assembled the senate; and, at the instance of his friends, who had been tutored for the purpose, this assembly bestowed upon him the government of Lucca for life, with the title of prince. He afterwards caused this grant to be confirmed by an assembly of the people; his warlike achievements, joined to the moderate expenditure of his government, had made him a great favourite with the inferior classes of the community, and they cordially entered into the projects of his ambition. Soon after, through the mediation of his friend Galeazzo Visconti, he obtained from Frederic, king of the Romans, the dignity of Imperial Vicar in Tuscany.

All this passed during the winter; and in the spring he assembled his troops, intent upon some new design. He had now been at peace with Florence for the space of three years, although, fighting under opposite banners, the spirit of enmity had always subsisted between him and them. Now, without declaring war, or in any way advising them of their peril, he suddenly made an incursion into their territory, burning and wasting their land as far as Empoli, taking several castles, and carrying off an immense booty; he then retreated back to Lucca.

This violation of every law of nations filled the Florentines at first with affright, and afterwards with indignation. They had sent their best troops to Genoa; and they found themselves attacked without warning or time for preparation. When the Lucchese retreated, anger and complaint succeeded. Castruccio replied to the reproaches of the Florentines by a declaration of war, and then immediately marched with his forces to join the besieging army before Genoa.

When the Florentines found that they could obtain no redress, they turned their thoughts to revenge. They raised what fresh troops they could among the citizens; and wishing to assist their small army by other measures which were then rife in the Italian system of warfare, they endeavoured to foment a conspiracy among the Lucchese for the overthrow of their prince's government. Castruccio received in one day letters from Giovanni da Castiglione, the general who commanded the few troops which he had left to guard his own principality, to inform him, that the Florentines had entered the Val di Nievole, burning and spoiling every thing before them; and from Vanni Mordecastelli, his civil lieutenant at Lucca, with information of a plot for the destruction of his power which was brewing in that city. Castruccio immediately left the Lombard army, and returned with his troops to disconcert these designs.

Of the castles which were situated within a circuit of many miles round Lucca, all were subject to Castruccio, except the castle of Valperga and its dependencies. He had often solicited Euthanasia to place her lordship under the protection of his government; and she had uniformly refused. The castle of Valperga was situated on a rock, among the mountains that bound the pass through which the Serchio flows, and commanded the northern entrance to the Lucchese territory. It was a place of great strength, and in the hands of an enemy might afford an easy entrance for an hostile army into the plain of Lucca itself. The Florentines, trusting to the affection which the countess bore their city, sent ambassadors to her to intreat her to engage in an alliance with them against Castruccio, and to admit a party of Florentine soldiers into her castle; but she rejected their proposals, and positively refused to enter into any league injurious to the existing government of Lucca. The ambassadors had been selected from among her intimate friends;

and her *Monualdo*, Bondelmonti, was at the head of them: they were not therefore intimidated by one repulse, but reiterated their arguments, founded upon her own interest, and the service she would render to her native town, in vain. She felt that the liberty in which she had been permitted to remain, while, one after another, all the castles around her had been reduced, could only have arisen from the friendship and forbearance of the prince; and she judged that it would be a sort of treason in her, to take advantage of his moderation to introduce devastation into his country; at the same time she promised, that no threats or intreaties should induce her to ally herself with, or submit to, the enemy of Florence.

The ambassadors, who had been bred in the Italian school of politics of that age, little understood, and by no means approved her scruples; they found her however invincible to their arguments, and were obliged to give up all expectation of her assistance. But they made the hope of overcoming her objections the pretext for their protracted stay in her castle; for they had other designs in view. The vicinity of Valperga to Lucca, and the intercourse which took place between it and that town, gave them an opportunity of becoming acquainted with several of the discontented nobles, the remnants of the faction of the *Neri*, who had been permitted to remain. Euthanasia, being a Guelph, had of course much intercourse with the few of that party who were to be found in Lucca; and from the conversation of these men the Florentine ambassadors conceived the hope of weaving some plot which would produce the downfal of Castruccio. And they believed, that in one of them they had found a successor to his dignity, and a chief who would prove as faithful to the papal party, as Castruccio had been to the imperial.

Among those of the faction of the *Neri* who had remained in Lucca, was a branch of the family of Guinigi, and one of the youths of this house had married Lauretta dei Adimari, a cousin of Euthanasia. This connexion had caused great intimacy between the families; and Leodino de' Guinigi, the husband of Lauretta, was a young man of talent, spirit and ambition. Being refused a command in the army of Castruccio, he was however forced to expend his love of action and his desire of distinction, in hunting, hawking and tournaments. He was a man of large fortune, and greatly respected and loved in Lucca; for his manners were courteous, and his disposition generous, so that every one blamed the prince for neglecting a person of so much merit on account of his party. Every year however added to the discontent of Leodino; and he used frequently at the castle of his cousin Euthanasia, to bemoan his fate, and declare how he longed for a change which should draw him from idleness and obscurity. Lauretta was a beautiful and amiable girl; but, party feelings ran so high in Lucca, that she was shunned as a Guelph and a Florentine, and therefore she also entered eagerly into the complaints of her husband; while the fear of the confiscation of his property withheld Leodino from serving under some leader of his own party. Euthanasia esteemed him highly; his mind was greatly cultivated; and the similarity of their tastes and pursuits had given rise to a sincere affection and sympathy between them. The Florentine ambassadors saw Leodino and his wife at the castle of Valperga; they easily penetrated his character and wishes; and Bondelmonti undertook to work on him to co-operate with them in their design. Leodino required little instigation, and immediately set to work in Lucca to gain partizans: every thing promised well. All this had been carefully concealed from Euthanasia; who was too sincere of disposition to suspect fraud in others. But their plot was now ripe; and the ambassadors were on the eve of returning to Florence to lead their troops to the attack; when the conspiracy was betrayed to Mordecastelli, and Castruccio suddenly appeared in Lucca.

Bondelmonti and his associates instantly quitted Valperga; and several of the conspirators, struck with affright, fled from Lucca; but Leodino, trusting to the secrecy with which he had enveloped his name, resolved to brave all danger and to remain. This imprudence caused his destruction; and, the morning after the return of Castruccio, he and six more of his intimate associates were arrested, and thrown into prison. Lauretta fled in despair to the castle of Valperga; she threw herself into the arms of Euthanasia, confessed the plot that had been carried on with Bondelmonti, and intreated her intercession with the prince to save the life of Leodino. Euthanasia felt her indignation rise, on discovering that her hospitality had been abused, and her friendship employed as the pretence which veiled a conspiracy. But, when the weeping Lauretta urged the danger of Leodino, all her anger was changed into compassion and anxiety; and she ordered the horses to be brought to the gate, that she might hasten to Lucca. "I am afraid, my poor cousin," said she, "if the prince be not of himself inclined to mercy, that my intreaties will have little effect: but be assured that I will spare no prayers to gain the life of Leodino. His life! indeed that is far too precious to be lightly sacrificed; I feel a confidence within me, which assures me that he will be saved; fear nothing, therefore; I will bring him back with me when I return."

She had covered her head with her veil, and folded her capuchin round her; when an attendant announced the arrival of Castruccio himself at the castle. This unexpected news made her turn pale; and again the blood, flowing from her heart, dyed her cheeks and even her fingers with pink; she hardly knew what caused her agitation; but she trembled, her eyes filled with tears, her voice faultered;—Castruccio entered.

He was no longer her lover, scarcely her friend; no joy sparkled in the eyes of either at this meeting after a separation of months; she had loved him passionately, and still dwelt with tenderness on the memory of what he had been; but she saw no likeness between the friend of her youth, beaming with love, joy and hope, and the prince who now stood before her; his brow was bent, his curved lips expressed disdain, his attitude and gesture were haughty and almost repulsive. Euthanasia was not to be daunted by this shew of superiority; she instantly recovered her presence of mind, and advanced towards him with calm dignity, saying, "My lord, I was about to visit you, when I find that you prevent me by honouring my castle with your presence; I was coming as a suppliant for the life of a dear friend."

"Countess, perhaps my errand is of more serious import,—at least to yourself: and, since it may include an answer to your supplication, I intreat you to hear me before we enter on any other subject."

Euthanasia bowed assent, and Castruccio continued.

"Madonna, you may remember that I have often in friendly terms intreated you to place yourself under the protection of my government at Lucca; you have ever refused me, and I indulgently acceded to your refusal. I have subdued all the castles around, several stronger than this, but I have left you to enjoy the independence you prized. I did this, trusting to your promise, that, although you were not my ally, you would not become my enemy, and that, in whatever war I might engage myself, you would preserve a strict neutrality. On my return from Genoa, forced to this hasty measure by the intimation of a plot being formed against me, I find that you are at the head of my enemies, and that, in violation of your faith, if you have not declared war, you have acted a more injurious part, in fomenting a conspiracy, and giving traitors those opportunities for maturing their plans, which, unless you had done this, they could never have dreamed of."

Euthanasia replied earnestly; "My lord, your mistake would be pardonable, had you not known me long enough to be assured that I am incapable of acting the part you attribute to me. But, although you have forgotten that treason and artifice are as foreign to my nature as darkness to that of the sun, you will at least believe me, when I give you my solemn assurance, that until this morning I knew nothing of the conspiracy entered into against you. And now"——

"But how can this be? Did not Bondelmonti and his associates reside in this castle for two months?"

"They did; they came to urge me to enter into the Florentine war against you, which I refused."

"And was it necessary to hesitate during two months for your answer? or, did it not rather enter into your plans, that they should remain as spies and plotters for my destruction? but enough of this"——

"Enough, and far too much, my lord. You doubt my faith, and disbelieve my word: these are outrages which I did not expect to receive from you, but to which I must submit. And now permit me to speak to you on the subject of my intended visit."

"Pardon me, but you may remember that we agreed I should be the first heard; and I have not yet mentioned why I intrude myself into your castle. I am at war with Florence; you are not; and you believe yourself permitted, not only to hold correspondence with my enemies, but also to afford them an opportunity through your means to carry on plots with my traitorous subjects. This may have been done very innocently on your part; but I cannot permit a repetition of the same mime, or of any other, which, though differing in words, shall be the same in spirit. If you have not taken advantage of my forbearance, you have at least shewn yourself incapable of sustaining the trust I reposed in you. But, Euthanasia, if you are indeed innocent, I am unmannerly in being thus stern with you; and, since you deny that you entered into this plot, and I would fain believe you, it is with repugnance that I enter upon the subject of my visit. You must surrender your castle to me; prudence no longer permits me to suffer you to enjoy independence; and, however painful the alternative, you must submit to become my ally."

"It were of little moment to enter into a treaty with me," said Euthanasia, with a bitter smile: "since, if I am capable of treason, I may be more dangerous as an ally than an enemy."

"Not so; for the first article of our alliance must be the razing of this castle; in exchange you shall have a site afforded you in the plain for the erection of a palace, nor shall you incur any loss in fortune or revenue; but you must descend to the rank of a private individual, and this castle, and your power in this country, must be resigned into my hands."

"My lord, I am afraid that we shall not agree on the first article of our intended treaty. I will persevere in the neutrality I promised, and endeavour to be more prudent than I was in this last unfortunate affair. But I cannot surrender my castle, or permit the seat of my ancestors to be razed to the ground. And now allow me to speak of what is nearer to my heart. Leodino de' Guinigi has conspired against you, you have discovered his plot, and have thrown him into prison. I know that you consider his life a forfeit to your laws; but I intreat you to spare him: if neither the generosity of your character, nor the impotence of your enemy will incline you to mercy, I intreat you by our antient friendship. His wife, Lauretta dei Adimari, is my cousin, and my friend; Leodino, although your enemy, is a man distinguished by every virtue, brave, generous and wise. If you would obtain a faithful and trust-worthy friend, pardon him, confide in him; and his gratitude will be to you as a guard an hundred strong: if you have not sufficient magnanimity to trust your enemy, banish him; but for my sake spare his life."

Castruccio appeared somewhat moved by her earnestness, but he replied;—"It cannot be; I am sorry to refuse you, but the example would be too dangerous. Put aside this from your thoughts, and let me in treat you to consider what I have just said. You answer me slightly; but be assured that I have not mentioned this alternative of war or peace between us, until my purpose was fixed: reflect seriously on the evils that resistance may bring upon you, and send me your answer to-morrow."

"To-morrow, or to-day, it is the same. But you, Castruccio, reflect upon the misery you cause, if you refuse to spare my unfortunate friend."

"Do not torment yourself or me any more on the subject of Leodino; your intercession is fruitless; he is already dead; I gave orders for his immediate execution before I left Lucca.—But why are you so pale?—What agitates you?"

Euthanasia could not speak; the horror that she felt on hearing the violent death of one she loved announced so coldly by his murderer, overcame her: she struggled violently not to faint; but, when Castruccio drew near to support her, he found her hand cold and lifeless; and her trembling limbs alone shewed that she still felt: her lips were pale; she stood as if changed to stone:—

"Euthanasia, speak!"

"Speak! What should I say? Leave me! You touch me, and your hands are covered with blood, your garments are dripping with gore; come not near me!—Oh! God, have pity on me, that I should know this misery! Leave me; you are not a man; your heart is stone; your very features betray the icy blood which fills your veins. Oh, Leodino!"

And then she wept, and her features relaxed from the rigid horror they had expressed into softness and grief. After she had wept awhile, and thus calmed her agitation, she said: "My lord, this is the last time that we shall ever meet. You may attack my castle, if you will; you may tear it down, and leave not a stone to shew where it stood; but I will never voluntarily submit to a tyrant and a murderer. My answer is brief;—Do your worst: it cannot be so bad as that which you have already done! You have destroyed every hope of my life; you have done worse, far worse, than my words can express; do not exasperate me, or let me exasperate you, by a longer stay: I can never forgive the death of Leodino; farewell!—we are enemies; do your worst against me."

She left him, unable to retain any longer even the patience to behold him. But she had no leisure afforded her to indulge her grief or indignation.

Lauretta had heard of the death of her husband; and her despair, and the convulsions it occasioned, entirely engrossed Euthanasia's attention, so that she forgot her own feelings and situation; nor did she recur to the threats of Castruccio, until they were recalled to her recollection by other proceedings on his part.

He did not doubt in his own mind, that, when pushed to extremity, the countess would surrender her castle. When he first heard that it had been selected by the conspirators as their rendezvous, he believed that she had had a principal share in the plot; but now, when assured of her innocence (for it was impossible not to believe her words, so clearly were truth and courageous sincerity painted on her noble countenance), he did not for that relent in his purpose of depriving her of the independence that she possessed, in the midst of a territory subject to himself. Like many of his predecessors and successors in usurpation, Castruccio had a method in his tyranny; and he never proceeded to any act of violence, without first consulting with his council, and obtaining their sanction to his measures. On his return from the castle of Valperga, he called together this friendly assembly, and represented to them the evil he incurred by permitting so violent a Guelph as the countess Euthanasia, to preserve her power, and erect her standard, in the very heart of his principality. His council replied to his representations with one voice, that the castle must be reduced.

The following morning Castruccio bade Arrigo di Guinigi carry a message to Euthanasia. Arrigo had always been a favourite with the countess; and Castruccio thought that it would be more delicate and forbearing, to send one so young and unpresuming as the bearer of his most displeasing message. Euthanasia received the youth with kindness; they talked on various subjects; but she carefully refrained from mentioning Castruccio's name, or alluding to the late transactions at Lucca; and it was long before Arrigo could summon courage to introduce the topic himself; at length he said:

"Madonna, I bear a message to you from the prince."

Euthanasia changed colour when he was alluded to; he, whom she now feared, as formerly she had dwelt on his idea with love. She replied hastily; "What is Antelminelli's pleasure with me? Speak quickly, that there may soon be an end of a subject, which I cannot even think upon without agitation."

"Yet I must intreat your patience, for my message is neither short nor unimportant; and you must pardon me that I am its bearer: you know by what ties I am bound to Castruccio; and if I now obey him, do not, dearest countess, condemn me too harshly. He intreats you to remember what he said when he visited you two days ago; he has since discussed the affair in council; and it is agreed that you can no longer be permitted to retain your independence. You know that the prince is all-powerful here; his army is well disciplined and formidable; his commands every where submitted to unquestioned. Look at every castle and village for miles around; they acknowledge his law; you cannot dream therefore of resisting; and, if you refuse to submit, it is because you believe that he will not proceed to extremities with you. My dear Euthanasia, this is a grievous task for me, and one which no earthly power but Castruccio could have persuaded me to undertake; pardon me, if I appear unmannerly when I repeat his words.

"He says, that he does not forget the friendship that once subsisted between you, and that he deeply regrets that your coldness and violence caused a division between you; but this is a question of state, and not a private altercation; and he would be unworthy of the trust reposed in him, if he permitted his individual inclinations to interfere with his duty towards the public. He is commanded by the ruling powers of his country, to compel the submission of the castle and rock of Valperga; and he is resolved to obey them: he intreats you to spare both yourself and him the unhappiness you will inflict on him, and the blood that must be shed, if you resist. It would be absurd to attempt to defend yourself alone: to give your cause the least chance of success you must call in foreign aid; and, by bringing the Florentines into the heart of this valley, you not only introduce war and destruction into the abodes of peace, but you act a treasonable part (forgive me if I repeat his word), in taking advantage of the power which you hold through his indulgence, to endeavour to bring ruin upon him. But, whatever you determine upon, whether to hold out with your own small forces, or to call strangers to your assistance, he is resolved to spare no exertion, and to be stopped by no obstacle, until he has reduced into his own hands Valperga and all its dependencies; at the same time that you, so far from being a loser, except in nominal advantages, shall be fully compensated for your present possessions."

Euthanasia listened attentively, although sometimes disdain hovered on her lips, and at times her eyes flashed fire at the words she heard. She paused a moment to collect her thoughts, and then she replied: "My dear Arrigo, I pardon most freely all the part you take in these unfortunate circumstances; I would that the prince had not so far degraded himself, as to veil his tyranny with hypocrisy and falsehood; his is the power, and not the senate's; to him I reply; and, casting away all the vain pretexts with which he would hide, perhaps to himself, his injustice and lawless ambition, I reply with plain words to his artful speech; and I beg that without any alteration you faithfully deliver my message to him.

"I will never willingly surrender my power into his hands: I hold it for the good of my people, who are happy under my government, and towards whom I shall ever perform my duty. I look upon him as a lawless tyrant, whom every one ought to resist to the utmost of their power; nor will I through cowardice give way to injustice. I may be exasperated beyond prudence; but right is on my side: I have preserved the articles of my alliance with him, and I will hold them still; but, if he attack me, I shall defend myself, and shall hold myself justified in accepting the assistance of my friends. If I had not that right, if indeed I had pledged myself to submit whenever he should call upon me to resign my birthright, what an absurd mockery is it to talk of his moderation towards me! I acknowledge that he might long ago have attempted, as now he threatens, to reduce this castle to a frightful ruin; but then I should have resisted as I shall now; resisted with my own forces, and those of my allies. Valperga stands on a barren rock, and the few villages that own its law are poor and unprotected; but this castle is as dear to me as all his dominion is to him; I inherited it from my ancestors; and if I wished to despoil myself of power, it would be to make my people free, and not to force them to enter the muster-roll of a usurper and a tyrant.

"My dear Arrigo, do not endeavour to persuade me to alter my purpose; for it is fixed. I am not young nor old enough to be scared by threats, nor happy enough to buy life on any terms Castruccio may choose to offer. I am willing to lose it in a just cause; and such I conceive to be the preservation of my inheritance."

Arrigo was too raw and inexperienced to contend in words with Euthanasia; he was overcome by her enthusiasm, which, although serious and apparently quiet, was as a stream that runs deep and waveless, but whose course is swifter and stronger than that which wastes its force in foam and noise.

CHAPTER X

Castruccio reconnoitres for a Surprise.—Embassy of Tripalda.

Arrigo returned sorrowfully to Lucca. He found Castruccio playing at chess with Mordecastelli; while a priest, Battista Tripalda, sat observing the game, and spoiling it by his interference.

"Nay, Vanni, I shall check-mate you next move," said Castruccio; "think again if you cannot escape, and make better play. Well, Arrigo, is peace or war the word you bring?"

"You must choose that, my lord; the countess wishes for peace, but she will not submit."

"Not submit!" cried Tripalda, stalking with his tall, upright figure into the middle of the room. "The woman is mad! I see that there is something wrong in this, that I must set right."

"Aye," said Mordecastelli; "as you set my game right for me, and made me lose two knights and a castle."

"I wish he could persuade Euthanasia to lose a castle, and then all would go well. Are there no hopes, Arrigo? tell me what she said."

Arrigo repeated her message, endeavouring to soften her expressions; but Castruccio was too experienced in the management of the human mind, not to draw from the youth the very words she had uttered.

"A murderer and a tyrant! pretty words applied to me, because I put a traitor to death, who otherwise would have placed my head on a Florentine pike. To what extremities am I driven! I would give the world not to go to open war about her miserable castle: yet have it I must, and that quickly, before she can send for her Florentine friends. What a spirit she has! I do not blame her; but, by St. Martin, I must tame it! Vanni, send for Castiglione; I must give him instructions for the conduct of the siege: I will have nothing to do with it personally; so to-morrow I shall away to keep the Florentines in check, if not to beat them."

"My lord," said Tripalda, drawing himself up before Castruccio with an air of the utmost self-consequence, "you have often found me of use in occasions of this sort; and I intreat you to authorize me to go and expostulate with the countess; I doubt not that I shall bring you a favourable answer: she must hear reason, and from no one is she so likely to hear it as from myself."

"You little know her disposition, friend Tripalda; but the most hopeless effort is worth making, before I declare war, and take her possessions by force. Go therefore to-morrow morning early; in the mean time I will give Castiglione my instructions; that, if your persuasions are vain, he may commence the attack the following day."

Tripalda then retired to meditate the speech by which he should persuade Euthanasia to yield; while Castruccio, desperate of any composition, gave his full directions for the conduct of the siege.

"If I were not in the secret of the place," said he to Castiglione, "I might well believe the castle of Valperga to be impregnable, except by famine; and that would be a tedious proceeding; but I know of other means which will give you entrance before nightfall. Lead a detachment of your most useless soldiers to the pathway which conducts to the main entrance of the castle; that of course will be well guarded; and, if the defence is directed with common judgement, the disadvantages under which the assailants must labour would render the attempt almost insane. But, as I said, let your more useless troops be employed there; they will keep the besieged in play; while you will conduct a chosen band to sure victory. You remember the fountain of the rock, beside which we were feasted, when the countess held her court, and where she sustained the mockery of a siege; to be conquered in play, as she now will be in earnest. You remember the narrow path that leads from the fountain to the postern, a gate, which, though strong, may easily be cut through by active arms and good hatchets. I know a path which leads from this valley to the fountain; it is long, difficult, and almost impracticable; but I have scaled it, and so may you and your followers. To-night before the moon rises, and it rises late, we will ride to the spot, and when you are in possession of this secret, the castle is at your mercy."

It was now the beginning of the month of October; the summer, which had been particularly sultry, had swiftly declined; already the gales which attend upon the equinox swept through the woods, and the trees, who know

His voice, and suddenly grow grey with fear,
And tremble and despoil themselves,

had already begun to obey the command of their ruler: the delicate chesnut woods, which last dare encounter the blasts of spring, whose tender leaves do not expand until they may become a shelter to the swallow, and which first hear the voice of the tyrant Libeccio, as he comes all conquering from the west, had already changed their hues, and shone yellow and red, amidst the sea-green foliage of the olives, the darker but light boughs of the cork trees, and the deep and heavy masses of ilexes and pines. The evening was hot; for the Libeccio, although it shuts out the sun with clouds, yet brings a close and heavy air, that warms, while it oppresses.

When evening came, Castruccio and his companion addressed themselves for their expedition. They muffled themselves in their capuchins, and, leaving the town of Lucca, crossed the plain, riding swiftly and silently along. Who can descend into the heart of man, and know what the prince felt, as he conducted Castiglione to the secret path, discovered by his love, now used to injure and subdue her whom he had loved? The white walls of the castle, half concealed by the cork and ilex trees which grew on the platform before it, stood quietly and silent; and she who dwelt within, whose heart now beat fast with fear and wretchedness, was the lovely and beloved Euthanasia, whose sweet and soft eyes, which shone as violets beneath a load of snow, had formerly beamed unutterable love on him, and whose gentle and modulated voice had once pronounced words of tenderness, which, though changed, he could never forget,—it was she, the beautiful, who had lived on earth as the enshrined statue of a divinity, adorning all places where she appeared, and adored by all who saw her; it was she, whose castle he was about to take and raze, it was against her that he now warred with a fixed resolution to conquer. Castruccio thought on all this; he called to mind her altered mien, and the coldness which had changed her heart from a fountain of burning love to an icy spring: and this awakened a feeling which he would fain have believed to be indignation. "Shall this false girl," he muttered, "enjoy this triumph over me? And shall the love which she despises, save her from the fate to which her own coldness and imprudence consign her? Let her yield; and she will find the Castruccio whom she calumniates, neither a tyrant nor a monster; but, if she resist, on her be the burthen of the misery that must follow."

Yet still, as officious conscience brought forward excuses for her, and called on him again and again to beware, he rode along side Castiglione, and entered into conversation. "To-morrow at this hour," he said, "you and your troop must come along this road, and hide yourselves in the forest which we are about to enter. When morning is up, do not long delay to scale the mountain, and enter the castle, for the sooner you take it, the less blood will be shed: order the battle so, that the troops you leave for the false attack may be fully engaged with the besieged before you enter; and then, coming behind the garrison, you can drive them down the mountain among their enemies, so that they may all be taken prisoners, at small expence either of their lives or ours."

They now dismounted; and, leaving their horses to their servants, began to ascend the acclivity. They moved cautiously along; and, if there had been any to listen to their footsteps, the sound was drowned by the singing of the pines, which moaned beneath the wind. Following the path of a torrent, and holding by the jutting points of rock, or the bare and tangled roots of the trees that overhung them, they proceeded slowly up the face of the mountain. Then turning to the right, they penetrated a complete wilderness of forest ground, where the undergrowth of the giant trees, and the fern and brambles, covered every path, so that Castruccio had need of all his sagacity to distinguish the slight peculiarities of scene that guided him. They awoke the hare from her form; and the pheasants, looking down from the branches of the trees, flew away with a sharp cry, and the whiz of their heavy wings, as their solitude was disturbed.

Their progress was difficult and slow; but, after their toil had continued nearly two hours, Castruccio exclaimed, "Yes, I see that I am right!" and he paused a moment beside a spring, near which grew a solitary, but gigantic cypress, that seemed, as you looked up, to attain to the bright star which shone right above it, and towards which its moveless spire pointed; "I am right; I know this place well; mark it, Castiglione; and now our journey is almost ended."

It was here, that in their childish days Castruccio and Euthanasia often played; their names were carved on the rough bark of the cypress, and here, in memory of their infantine friendship, they had since met, to renew the vows they had formerly made, vows now broken, scattered to the winds, more worthless than the fallen leaves of autumn on which he then trod. The way to the rock which overlooked the fountain was now short, but more difficult than ever; and both hands and feet were necessary to conquer the ascent. At length they came to a pinnacle, which, higher than the castle, overlooked the whole plain; and immediately under was the alcove which sheltered Euthanasia's fountain.

"I see no path which may lead to the fountain, my lord," said Castiglione.

"There is none," replied the prince, "nor did I ever get into the castle this way; but I have observed the place, and doubt not of the practicability of my plan."

Castruccio drew from under his cloak a rope, and fastened it to the shattered stump of a lightning-blasted tree; by the help of this rope, and a stick shod with iron which he carried in his hand, he contrived with the aid of Castiglione to reach a projecting ledge in the rock about two feet wide, which ran round the precipice about ten feet from its base; the fountain flowed from a crevice in this ledge, and steps were hewn out of the rock, leading from the source to the basin. Castruccio pointed out these circumstances to his companion, and made it fully apparent that, with a little boldness and caution, they might arrive by the means he had pointed out at the path which led to the postern of the castle. A few questions asked by Castiglione, which the prince answered with accuracy and minuteness, sufficed to clear all the doubts which the former had entertained, and to explain the whole of his proceeding.

As they returned, however, Castiglione said suddenly, "My lord, you understand this path so much better than I, why will you not undertake the attack?"

"I thank you," replied Castruccio, with a bitter smile; "but this business falls to your share; I must away to keep off the aid the countess expects from the Florentines."

They descended slowly; the moon had risen, which would have discovered their path to them, but that she was hid behind so thick a woof of dark and lightning-bearing clouds, that her presence sufficed only to dispel the pitchy blackness, in which, but for her, they had been enveloped. Every now and then the growling of distant but heavy thunder shook the air, and was answered by the screeching of the owl, and the screams of the birds whom it awoke from their sleep among the trees. The two adventurers soon reached the valley; and, mounting their horses, crossed the plain at full gallop; and the strong Libeccio against which they drove, cutting the air with difficulty, warmed the spirits, and somewhat dissipated the melancholy, which, in spite of all his efforts, oppressed Castruccio. He arrived much fatigued at his journey's end; and, whatever might be the revolutions in his feelings, or the remorse which stung him when he reflected on the work for which he prepared, throwing himself on his couch, deep sleep quickly overcame all; nor did he awake, until an attendant came to announce to him, that the day was advanced, that the troops had long quitted Lucca, and that his principal officers, waited only for him to join them in their march towards the Florentine camp. Castruccio then shook off sleep; and, having examined well that his esquire had omitted no piece of his armour which another horse bore, and having visited his charger which was to be led unbacked to the field, he mounted a black palfrey; and, merely saying to Castiglione, as he passed him in the palace court, "You understand all,"—he joined his officers, and they rode off on the road to Florence.

As they quitted the town, they met Tripalda, who, accosting the prince, told him, that he was now going to Valperga, and that he did not doubt that his arguments would induce the countess to surrender. Castruccio shook his head in disbelief, and, hastily wishing him good-success, put spurs to his horse, apparently impatient to quit every thing that reminded him of the odious task he had left his friends to perform.

Battista Tripalda, the ambassador of Castruccio on this occasion, was a canon of the cathedral of St. Ambrose at Perugia. By this time the colleges of canons, who had before lived in common like monks, had been dissolved, and each member was permitted to live privately, receiving his share of the yearly income which was before employed as a common stock. But the canons had offices to perform in the church, which obliged them to reside in the town, in which the cathedral to which they belonged was situated; Tripalda had however been long absent from his duties, nor did his bishop ever enquire after him, or require him to return. He had appeared at Lucca about a year before this time, unknown and unrecommended; but he had intruded himself into the palaces of the nobles, and been well received: his eccentric manners made them pardon his opinions, and the subtleties of his mind forced them to forgive his uncouth and arrogant demeanour. Yet, although received by all, he was liked by none, for there was a mystery about him that no one could divine; and we seldom like what we do not comprehend. He was an unbelieving priest, yet was permitted to exercise the clerical functions; he was a man who cried out against the simony and wickedness of the Roman religion, yet he was tolerated by all its members; he was equally severe against tyrants and lords, yet he was received at every court in Italy. He was an earnest panegyrizer of republics and democracies; yet he was satisfied with no existing form of government, because none was sufficiently free: he contended that each man ought to be his own king and judge; yet he pretended to morality, and to be a strict censor of manners and luxury. He had a deep insight into artful and artificial character, and a kind of instinctive prudence in extricating himself from the most embarrassing circumstances; so that his penetration almost gave him the appearance of a tamperer in the forbidden arts, which however he held in supreme contempt.

He was equally well received by the opposite factions, allying himself with neither, but condemning both. When he first appeared at Lucca, he was humble and mild, pretending to nothing but uncorrupted and uncorruptible virtue, desiring none of the goods of fortune, except that which she could not withhold from him, namely, the esteem and friendship of all good men. But this was merely the prelude to what was to follow. He was as those dwarfs we read of in fairy tales, who at first appear small and impotent, but who on further acquaintance assume the form of tremendous giants; so, when he became familiar with his new friends, he cast off his modest disguise, and appeared vain, presumptuous and insolent, delivering his opinions as oracles, violent when opposed in argument, contemptuous even when agreed with: there was besides something buffoonish in his manner, which he occasionally endeavoured to pass off for wit and imagination, and at other times, served him as a cloak for deep designs and dangerous opinions. The Guelphs declared that they believed him to be a Ghibeline spy; the Ghibelines, that he was under pay from the Pope; many said, that he tampered with both parties, and betrayed both. Worse stories had been whispered concerning him, but they were believed by few; it was said that the flagrant wickedness of his actions had caused him to be banished from

Perugia; but this was disproved at once, for if so, why was he not deprived of his emoluments in the church?

The first conjecture concerning him was that he was a spy; but, however that might be, he escaped detection, and contrived to maintain his confidence with the chiefs of the opposite factions, and among these was Euthanasia. She admired his talents, believed him to be honest, and refused to listen to the accusations advanced against him, since the manner in which they were brought forward stamped them with the show of unfounded calumnies. She was sometimes irritated by his impertinence, and shocked at his want of delicacy; but she had heard that early misfortunes had deranged his understanding, and she pitied and forgave him. Indeed she had known him a very short time; and he had not yet thrown off his mask of humility and virtue, which he ever wore on his first appearance on a new scene.

Euthanasia waited with impatience to hear the result of her message to Castruccio. She could not believe that he would put his threats in execution; but, in case of the worst, she resolved to oppose his pretensions, and to use every means to preserve her independence. She had sent, the same night of her interview with Arrigo, to intreat the Florentine general to dispatch a brigade for her defence, and to request the assistance of an able officer in sustaining the siege she might encounter. She called together the few militia of her villages. She visited the works of the castle, and gave orders for the immediate demolition of all roads and bridges on the first advance of the enemy; and then, overcome by the sense of wretchedness which clung to her in spite of the exalted state of her mind, she shrunk to solitude, and tried to seek in the recesses of her own soul for the long-studied lessons of courage and fortitude.

She believed herself justified, nay called upon to oppose the encroachments of the prince of Lucca; she felt roused to resistance by his menaces, and the implied accusation of treachery with which he had endeavoured to brand her. Her innocence made her proud, her spirit of independence, bold; she had ever refused to submit to his usurpations; her castle had often been the asylum for his victims, and herself the aider of the persecuted. "I may fall," she thought; "but I will not stoop. I may become his victim; but I will never be his slave. I refused to yield to him when I loved him, if he did not dismiss his ambitious designs. Love, which is the ruling principle of my mind, whose power I now feel in every nerve, in every beating of my heart, I would not submit my conscience to the control of love; and shall fear rule me?"

She said this, and at the same moment Tripalda was announced. He advanced towards Euthanasia with a serious and important look, yet at the same time with an endeavour to appear courteous, if not humble. He kissed her hand, and having gravely asked after her health, he soon began to speak on the object of his visit, and to endeavour to persuade her that all resistance to the will of the prince was useless, and that in timely submission was the only hope left for her preservation. Euthanasia felt her cheeks glow as he spoke, and once her eyes seemed to flash lightning, when the word *Mercy* escaped from the orator, who talked on, appearing to observe little of what she felt, but to be wholly engrossed in the winding up of his periods. "Madonna," said he, "the prince has a true and sincere friendship for you, and he is infinitely grieved at the idea of being at open hostility with you; but he must obey the will of the senate and the council, and you must ultimately submit to the forces sent against you. Listen then to one older than yourself, who has lived longer in the world, and has grown wise by experience: never, being, weak, contend with the strong; for it is far more politic to yield at first upon conditions, than, falling after combat, to receive the law from the conqueror."

"I am afraid, *Messer Canonico*," replied Euthanasia, calmly, but somewhat haughtily, "that our opinions agree too little, to allow you to be a fitting arbiter between me and the prince of Lucca. This castle, and the power annexed to it, belonged to my ancestors; and when I received it from my mother's hands, I vowed to exercise and preserve it for the good of my people——"

"And is it for the good of your people to expose them to the desolation of war, when you might conclude a satisfactory peace?"

"Messer Battista, I listened patiently while you spoke; and it boots little to continue this discussion, if you will not also attend to me. I will be very brief: Castruccio formed an alliance with me, and, as the condition of my independence, I promised not to join his enemies. I have preserved my part of the agreement; and, if he wishes to break his, I have friends and allies, who will not permit that my situation should be so hopeless as you imagine. It is the height of injustice to say that I bring war into this territory; since every prayer and every wish of my heart is for peace; but, if attacked, I will defend myself, and my right must become both my sword and shield."

"You speak proudly, but foolishly, countess Euthanasia; for right was never yet sword or shield to any one. It is well to talk in this manner to women and children, and thus to keep the world in some degree of order. You are a woman, it is true; but your rank and power have placed you in a situation to know the truth of things; and, if you have not yet learned the futility of the lessons of the priests, whose sole end to all their speeches is to find a way, shorter or longer, into your purse; learn it from me, who am both willing and able to teach you."

"I shall make a sorry pupil, I am afraid; but, if you please, I will alter my phraseology, that my meaning may be more clear. I expect the aid of the

Florentines; and I depend upon the courage with which the hatred of a usurper will inspire my soldiers, who love me, and will, I doubt not, defend me to the last drop of their blood: if my right cannot help me, my resolution shall. The prince of Lucca has called me, perhaps he believes me to be, a traitor; I am none to him, nor will I be to the party to which I belong. I promised my allies not to submit; and my word is sacred. Messer Battista, I doubt not that the motives which urged your visit, were honest, perhaps friendly; but cease to vex yourself and me with fruitless altercation."

"I do not intend altercation, Madonna; but I wished to expostulate with you, and to shew you the pit into which you seem obstinately resolved to fall. I know that the wisdom of all ages tells us, that women will have their will; I had hoped to find you superior to the foibles of your sex; and my mistake becomes my crime: for in truth you are as headstrong as a girl of fifteen, who hopes to cover her head with the nuptial veil. But I have set my heart on carrying this point with you, and will not be discouraged by a woman's eloquence or obstinacy."

"This is going too far," said Euthanasia, half angrily; "you imagine perhaps that I am already the slave of your lord, that you no longer preserve the respect which even then would be due to me. My mind is too full both of grief and anxiety, to string sentences together in answer to your arguments; but my purpose is firm, and you cannot shake it. If you come from the lord Castruccio himself, my answer is ever the same. I am at peace with him; but, if he attacks me, I know how to defend myself."

Any man but Tripalda might have been awed by the dignity of Euthanasia, and the restrained indignation, that glistened in her eyes, and flushed her cheek. She rose to bid the priest farewel, and her serious manner made him pause for an instant in his address; but his accustomed impudence quickly overcame the momentary shame, and he said, "I came to speak reason to the deaf, and to shew danger to the blind; but the deaf man says, I hear better than you, and the sound of arms and trumpets is yet far off;—and the blind man cries, Avaunt! I see my path better than you: meanwhile the one falls into the hands of the enemy, and the other tumbles into the pit round which I would have led him. You will repent too late, that you did not follow my counsel; and then who will medicine your wounds?"

"The God who inflicted them upon me. I fear not!"

Tripalda returned to Lucca. Castruccio had left the town; and Castiglione, hearing the result of the priest's embassy, instantly prepared for the attack. Heralds were sent in due form to demand the surrender of the castle; and, when refused, war was immediately declared.

In the mean time the Florentine army had advanced into the Lucchese territory; but, when they heard of the march of Castruccio, they fell back to Fucecchio, and pitched their tents on the banks of the river Guisciana. Castruccio came up to them with his troops; but, being on opposite sides of the river, and not caring to cross it in face of the enemy, both armies remained observing each other's motions, each preparing to attack the other on the first shew of fear or retreat. The Florentine general had received the message of Euthanasia, but he found it difficult to comply with her wishes; for any troops sent to her aid must pass the Guisciana, and that was too well guarded to permit of any but a general passage and attack. He communicated her situation to the Florentine government, which sent her a small troop with Bondelmonti at its head, who, making the circuit of Bologna and the Modenese mountains, arrived on the eve of the attack, having with infinite difficulty surmounted the fortified passages of the mountains; so that many of his followers being made prisoners, and others left behind, he made his appearance at Valperga with not more than fifty men.

CHAPTER XI

Valperga taken.

After the departure of Tripalda, Euthanasia remained long on the battlements of her castle, watching the men who were employed in repairing and erecting some outworks for its defence. Every now and then she heard a murmuring near her, a slight noise, and then a voice which said—"Aye, that will do; this helmet is still too large, I must find some way to cut it round the edges."

Looking up, she saw at a small window of one of the projecting towers the Albinois, who appeared furbishing and repairing arms. "Are we so straitened for men," she said, "that you are obliged to turn armourer, my poor Bindo?"

"Not an armourer, but a soldier, lady; to-morrow I gird on my sword for your defence."

"You, and a sword! Nay, that is impossible; you must not expose yourself to danger, where you can do no good."

"Countess, have firm hope; I have learned from the stars, that to-morrow is a fortunate day for us. I have visited the holy fountain; and, sprinkling its waters three times around, I have called on its saints to aid us: to-morrow is named as a lucky day for us, and I will be among your defenders."

He spoke earnestly; and so highly wrought were the feelings of Euthanasia, that, although at another time she might have smiled, she could now with difficulty repress her tears. "If you would defend me," she replied, "wait then near me; I will not indeed have you risk your life to no end."

"Why, Madonna," said Bindo, "should you care more for my life, than for those of the brave fellows who will to-morrow die for you? We shall succeed; but death will be among us; and to-morrow many a child will lose its father, and many a wife her husband, fighting for this heap of stones which can feel neither defeat nor triumph. I will be among them; fear not, St. Martin has declared for us."

There are moments in our lives, when the chance-word of a madman or a fool is sufficient to cause our misery; and such was the present state of Euthanasia's mind. She hastily retreated to solitude, and in earnest thought tried to overcome the effect of the conscience-stricken wound which the Albinois had inflicted. We are distrustful of ourselves; so little do we depend upon our human reason, that on the eve of any action, even the most praise-worthy, it will sometimes assume another semblance, and that will appear selfish wilfulness, or at best a distorted freak of the imagination, which, when we first contemplated it, seemed the highest effort of human virtue. It had appeared to Euthanasia her first duty to resist the incroachments of Castruccio, and to preserve the independence of her subjects. Now again she paused, and thought that all the shows this world presents were dearly bought at the price of one drop of human blood. She doubted the purity of her own motives; she doubted the justification which even now she was called upon to make at the tribunal of her conscience, and hereafter before that of her God; she stop, and shivered on the brink of her purpose, as a mighty fragment of rock will pause shaking at the edge of a precipice, and then fall to the darkness that must receive it.

"The earth is a wide sea," she cried, "and we its passing bubbles; it is a changeful heaven, and we its smallest and swiftest driven vapours; all changes, all passes—nothing is stable, nothing for one moment the same. But, if it be so, oh my God! if in Eternity all the years that man has numbered on this green earth be but a point, and we but the minutest speck in the great whole, why is the present moment every thing to us? Why do our minds, grasping all, feel as if eternity and immeasurable space were kernelled up in one instantaneous sensation? We look back to times past, and we mass them together, and say in such a year such and such events took place, such wars occupied that year, and during the next there was peace. Yet each year was then divided into weeks, days, minutes, and slow-moving seconds, during which there were human minds to note and distinguish them, as now. We think of a small motion of the dial as of an eternity; yet ages have past, and they are but hours; the present moment will soon be only a memory, an unseen atom in the night of by-gone time. A hundred years hence, and young and old we shall all be gathered to the dust, and I shall no longer feel the coil that is at work in my heart, or any longer struggle within the inextricable bonds of fate. I know this; but yet this moment, this point of time, during which the sun makes but one round amidst the many millions it has made, and the many millions it will make, this moment is all to me. Most willingly, nay, most earnestly, do I pray that I may die this night, and that all contention may cease with the beatings of my heart. Yet, if I live, shall I submit? Is all that we prize but a shadow? Are tyranny, and cruelty, and liberty, and virtue only names? Or, are they not rather the misery or joy, that makes our hearts the abode of storms, or as a smiling, flower-covered isle? Oh! I will no longer question my purpose, or waver where necessity ought to inspire me with courage. One heart is too weak to contain so overwhelming a contention."

While her melancholy thoughts thus wandered, and she seemed to range in idea through the whole universe, yet no where found repose, it was announced to her that Bondelmonti and his soldiers had arrived, and that the chief desired to see her. There was something in the name of Bondelmonti that struck a favourable chord in her heart; he had been her father's friend; he was her guardian, and, although she had sometimes run counter to his advice, yet she always felt most happy when his opinion coincided with hers. His presence thus announced seemed to cancel half her care; she collected all the courage she possessed, and that was a mighty store, and descended, even smiling, to the hall; her cares and regrets were leashed like dogs by the huntsmen, but they neither bayed nor yelled, but cowered in silence. Bondelmonti was struck by the serenity of her aspect; and his countenance changed from the doubt it had before expressed, to a frank and gallant address.

"Madonna," said he, "the work we undertake is difficult; Castruccio keeps our army in check, and guards the passes; and the fifty men that I bring you, is all out of three hundred that could pass the Serchio. Have good heart however, your castle walls are strong and will resist all the stones with which their *battifolle*[9] can batter it, if indeed they can scale the rock, which we must make as impracticable as we can. But this is not fitting work for you, fair countess; do you retire to rest; I would indeed that we could place you in safety in Florence out of all danger, where you would not be able to hear the clash of arms that to-morrow will resound in this castle. But I know that you have courage; and I now see all the calm fortitude of your father shine in your clear eyes; you are a good girl, Euthanasia, a good and a wise girl, and be assured that every drop of blood that warms my heart, every faculty of my body or my mind, are devoted to your cause."

Euthanasia thanked him in the warm language her feeling heart dictated, and he continued; "I should have much to say to you, much encouragement from your friends and messages of praise and affection; but my time is short: believe then in one word, that all your Florentine friends love, approve and admire you; and if you fall, which this good sword forbid, we shall at least have this consolation, that our long absent Euthanasia will reappear among us. But now to the works of war; I will apply to your seneschal to know what food you have in the castle, and what possibilities there are of increasing your stock; and your principal officers shall shew me your works of defence, that I may concert with them the plan for to-morrow's combat."

Euthanasia however undertook this task herself: she was too much agitated, not to find some relief in the shew of composure which she preserved with Bondelmonti, and in the exertion of explaining and pointing out the various modes of defence which she had adopted, in addition to those with which nature had furnished her habitation. The castle was built, as I have before said, on the projecting platform of a precipitous mountain: the wall of the edifice itself was thick and strong; and but a small way removed from it was a lower wall, built with corner towers and battlements, which at once defended the main building, and sheltered the besieged, who could shower stones and arrows on the assailants from the port-holes, and be in no danger of retaliation. Before the gate of the castle was a green plot, about fifteen paces across, planted with a few cork and ilex trees, and surrounded by a barbican or low wall built on the edge of the precipice, which, high, bare, and inaccessible, hung over the plain below. Between the wall and the barbican, a path ran round one side of the castle, which was terminated by massy gates and a portcullis; and it was there that, crossing the chasm which insulated the castle, by means of a drawbridge, you found the path that conducted to the plain. This path was defended by various works; palisades, wooden towers to shelter archers, and more by nature herself, for the rock and the trees were all so many asylums whence the defenders could uninjured prevent the approach of an enemy.

"This is all excellent," said Bondelmonti; "it is impossible that all the armies of Italy could force this pass, though it were defended only by a handful. But, Madonna, is there no other entrance to your castle? Is there no postern with a path up or down the mountain, whose secret your enemies may learn, and thus attack you unawares?"

"None; the only postern is that which opens on a path conducting to a small fountain about a hundred paces up the acclivity; but there it stops, and the rock rising precipitously behind forbids approach."

"It is well. I will now review your soldiers, appoint their various posts, and see that mine are refreshed; then, cousin, having tasted your wine, I will go to rest, that I may awake betimes to-morrow. I am resolved that all shall go well; Castruccio will be defeated; and you shall ever be, as you deserve, the castellana of Valperga."

The tables were spread in the great hall of the castle, and heaped with wine and food. After Euthanasia had seen every want of her guests supplied, she retired to her own room at the eastern angle of the castle, one window of which overlooked the whole plain of Lucca; and she sat near this window, unable to rest or sleep, in that breathless and feverish state, in which we expect a coming, but uncertain danger.

The veil of night was at length withdrawn; first Euthanasia saw the stars wax faint, and then the western sky caught a crimson tinge from the opposing sun. It was long ere he climbed the eastern hill; but his rays fell upon the opposite mountains, and the windows of the castle of Valperga shone dazzlingly bright. A *reveillée* was sounded in the court below, and roused the young countess from her waking dreams, to the reality that yawned as a gulph before her. First, she composed her dress, and bound the wandering locks of her hair round her head; then for a moment she stood, her hands folded on her bosom, her eyes cast up to heaven. At first her countenance expressed pain: but it changed; her pale cheek began to glow, her brow became clear from the cloud that had dimmed it, her eyes grew brighter, and her whole form gained dignity and firmness. "I do my duty," she thought, "and in that dear belief do I place my strength; I do my duty towards myself, towards my peasants, towards Castruccio, from whose hands I detain only the power of doing greater ill; God is my help, and I fear not."

Thinking and feeling thus, she descended to the hall of the castle; most of the soldiers had gone to their posts; but Bondelmonti, and some of those of higher rank in her party and household, were waiting her appearance. She entered not gaily, but serenely; and her beauty, the courage painted on her face, and her thrilling tone as she bade them good morrow, inspired them with a simultaneous emotion, which they almost expressed, and midway checked their voices. Bondelmonti kissed her hand; "Farewel, my friends," she said; "you risk your lives for me, and the sacrifice of mine were a poor recompense; my honour, my every hope rests upon your swords; they are wielded by those who love me, and I do not fear the result."

Bondelmonti addressed himself to the combat, ordered the men to their posts, and took his own station on the drawbridge of the castle. The winding path which led to the foot of the mountain, was lined with archers and slingers, who were hid behind the projecting rocks or trees, or within small wooden towers, erected for the purpose. A chosen band armed with long spears was stationed in firm array at the most precipitous part of the path, who, drawn up in close rank, and advancing their arms, formed an outwork of iron spikes, impossible to be passed or driven back. The foremost in the combat were the dependents of Euthanasia; they were full of that loud, but undisciplined courage which anger and fear inspire; Bindo was among them, and he harangued them, saying, that every sign in the heavens, and every power of air, was propitious to their mistress; at other times they had derided his superstition; but now it acted as another incentive to their indignation, and supporter for their courage.

In the mean time Euthanasia had retired to the apartment of Lauretta. This unfortunate lady had remained in the castle since the death of her husband; and such was the agony of grief she endured, that Euthanasia had not communicated to her the threats of Castruccio, and the approaching siege. The noise of arms, and the sound of many voices alarmed her; and she wildly asked the cause. Her friend related to her the events of the few last days, and endeavoured to calm her; Lauretta listened in fear; she had suffered so much by the like contentions, that every thing presented itself to her in the gloomiest point of view. Grasping the countess's hand, she intreated her to submit; "You know not what a siege is," she cried; "my father's castle was stormed, and therefore I well know. Even if Castruccio were at the head of his troops, he would in vain endeavour to restrain their fury; a triumphant soldier is worse than the buffalo of the forest, and no humanity can check his thirst for blood and outrage; they will conquer, and neither God nor man can save us."

Euthanasia tried to soothe her; but in vain. She wept bitterly, and prayed so earnestly that the countess would spare them both the utter misery they would endure, that Euthanasia was for a moment startled by her adjurations;

but then, recalling her thoughts, she replied with gentle firmness, and bade her lay aside her fears which were unfounded, for there was nothing to dread save an easy imprisonment, if they should be overcome.

And now, as they were talking thus, a messenger came from Bondelmonti. "The general desires you to have good heart," he said; "the troops of the enemy advance; and, if we may judge by their appearance, they are few, and even those few the refuse of the prince's army."

Euthanasia listened incredulously; for she knew that however doubtful the decision of the combat might be, the contention must be fierce. Soon the war-cry arose from without the castle, and was echoed from the walls and mountains; when it ceased, it was answered by the Ghibeline cry from the assailants. But this only proved the truth of Bondelmonti's assertion, that they were few, and of no note; for the shout was not that exhilarating sound, that echoes the soul's triumph, and, borne along the line, raises responsive ardour in every breast; it was loud, but soon died away.

Wearied by the childish remonstrances of Lauretta, Euthanasia descended to the platform of the castle, and leaned over the barbican; but she could see nothing, though her ears were stunned by the cries, and clash of arms, that rose from the valley. Returning to the inner court, she met some men who were bearing the wounded from the field, and bringing them for succour to the castle; for a moment her heart sunk within her, for a moment she was pierced with grief, as she thought—"This is my work!" But she recovered herself—"It must all be endured," said she; "I have undertaken a part, and will not faint on the threshold. Spirit of my father, aid me!"

Beds had been prepared in a large apartment of the castle, and Euthanasia mingled with the women who ministered to the wounded; she bound them with her own hands, cheered them with her voice, and endeavoured, by supporting their minds, to alleviate the sense of bodily pain. The men, who saw her flitting like an angel about them, aiding and ministering to their wants, felt all the love and gratitude that such unwonted, but gracious kindness might inspire. "Fear not, lady," they said; "we are even more numerous than those who attack us; already they are tired, and out of breath; fear not, the day is ours."

A messenger also came from Bondelmonti, to say, that the imprudence of an under-officer had caused the few to fall who had fallen, but that her troops were now all sheltered, and, that without the loss of a man they would either destroy all the assailants, or drive them down the steep; and this assertion appeared confirmed, since no more wounded were brought in. Thus reassured, Euthanasia left the hall, and ascended to her own apartment; her spirit was lightened of much of its burthen; the first barrier had been passed; and she feared not, she would not fear, the rest.

As she thought this, a sudden scream echoed through the castle; for a moment she was transfixed; the scream was repeated, louder and nearer, and she hastened to the window that overlooked the outer court. Thence she saw a party of soldiers in the Lucchese uniform issue from the gate, and run round the castle towards the drawbridge; as they came out in file she thought their numbers would never end, and she recognized several of the officers as those of the highest rank in Castruccio's army; the last at length disappeared, and she looked around for an explanation. The castle was silent; she stood alone in the room; and even the echo of footsteps reached her not: she paused a moment; and then, weary of further doubt, she hastened to the room of Lauretta, and found it full of soldiers,—the enemy's soldiers; while the poor girl, pale and trembling, sat bewildered and silent. Euthanasia entered from a small door, leading from a private staircase: her first words were addressed to her friend; "Fear not," she cried; "we are betrayed; but fear not."

The soldiers, seeing her appear, had sent for their chief officer, who came forward, saying, "The castle is ours; and, Madonna, it were well that you ordered your people to yield; for further resistance would be useless, and could only cause more bloodshed: we are commanded by our general to act with the greatest moderation."

"It is enough," replied Euthanasia, quietly; "the commander will judge of the necessity of submission: but see, you frighten this lady, who is ill and delicate. I beseech you to leave this room awhile; if I find that indeed no further resistance can be made, I shall soon be prepared to obey what orders you may bring."

"Madonna, we withdraw as you desire: but permit me to add, that it is the general's orders that we escort you to Lucca this evening: until then we shall not intrude upon you."

The soldiers quitted the room; and Euthanasia, leaving Lauretta with her servant, retired to her own apartment. Here she found several of her attendants, who told with many tears that there was no longer any hope; that the enemy, entering at the postern, had attacked her soldiers from behind, and driven them down the mountain, and that the party left in the castle having raised the drawbridge, were now in undisturbed possession. Euthanasia heard all this with an unaltered mien, and, when the melancholy tale was finished, she bade them leave her, and go to the commanding officer of the troop to receive orders for their further proceeding, but not to return to her, until she should command their attendance.

[9]*Battifolle*, or *balestri*, machines for casting stones.

CHAPTER XII

Euthanasia at Lucca.

The castle bell tolled the *Ave Maria* for the last time, answering the belfries of the various convents in the vale below. "There is my knell!" cried Euthanasia. At first she thought that it would please her, in quitting for ever the abode of her ancestors, to array herself in mourning garments; but then the simplicity of her mind made her instinctively shun any thing that had the appearance of affectation; so she covered her head with a white veil, folded her capuchin about her, and returned to the chamber of Lauretta to prepare for her removal. Castiglione sent thither to desire admittance; when he came, he felt awed by the deportment of Euthanasia, who received him with that slight tinge of pride mingled with her accustomed dignity, which adversity naturally bestows on the good. He announced that the escort had arrived to convey them to Lucca; Euthanasia bowed her head in acquiescence; and, supporting Lauretta, with an unfaltering step she left for the last time the castle of her ancestors; she supported her friend with one hand, and with the other folded her veil close to her face, that no rudely curious eye might read in its expression the sorrow that she felt in her heart. "My grief is my own," she thought; "the only treasure that remains to me; and I will hoard it with more jealousy from the sight and knowledge of others, than a miser does his gold."

She walked unhesitating through the hall, long the seat of her purest happiness. Her infant feet had trodden its pavement in unreproved gaiety; and she thought for a moment that she saw the venerable form of her father seated in his accustomed place. But she proudly shook the softening emotion from her, and looked with a tearless eye upon the hearth, round which the soldiers of her enemy stood, profaning its sacredness by their presence. The inner court of the castle was filled by a number of women and children, the wives of the peasantry who depended on her, who, as they saw her advance, raised one cry of grief; she started, and said in a smothered voice, "Could I not have been spared this?"

"Impossible," replied Castiglione, who overheard her; "nothing but the most brutal force could have prevented them."

"Enough," said Euthanasia; "I am satisfied."

The women clung about her, kissing her hands, her garments, and throwing themselves on their knees with all the violent gesticulation of Italians. They tore their hair, and called on heaven to save and bless their mistress, and to avenge her wrongs;—"God bless you, good people!" cried their countess;

"may you never be reminded of my loss by any misfortune that may befal yourselves!"

And, disengaging herself from their grasp, she walked on, while they followed crying and bewailing. She crossed the drawbridge, which was guarded at each end by soldiers; ere she put her foot on the opposite rock, Euthanasia paused for one moment; it seemed to her that all was irretrievably lost, when once she had passed the barrier which this bridge placed between her past and future life; she glanced back once more at the castle, and looked up to the window of her apartment; she had expected to find it desert and blank; but it was filled with soldiers, who stood looking from it on her departure; she sighed deeply, and then with quicker steps hastened down the mountain.

The idea that this path had been the scene of the morning's combat affrighted her; and she dared not look round, fearing that she might see some lifeless victim among the bushes and rocks on the road-side: and so it might easily have been; for, when Castiglione had ordered the road to be cleared of the dead, many had been cast behind the projections of rock, or under the low wood, in their haste; and, as they passed, the vulture arose from among the grass, scared from his prey, and told too truly that he feasted upon limbs which that same morning had been endowed with life. The very path on which she trod was slippery with blood; and she felt as if she walked through one of the circles of hell's torments[10], until she reached the foot of the rock.

Lauretta was placed in a litter; Euthanasia mounted her horse; and they prepared to depart: but the women again raising a cry, threw themselves about the horse, seizing the reins, and vowing that she should not leave them. "God bless you!" cried the poor countess, who, although filled with her own grief, yet sympathized with these good people; "but now go; you may harm yourselves with your new master; you can do no good to me."

The soldiers interfered; and, opening the path before Euthanasia, she gave the reins to her horse, and rode with speed out of the hearing of the cry, which her people again sent up, when they saw that she had indeed left them. She had outridden the rest of her party; and, finding herself alone, she drew up her palfrey to wait their arrival. She looked upon the castle, no longer hers; a few quick drops fell; she dried them again; and, seeing her escort approach, she turned her horse's head, and, without a word, proceeded slowly on her way to Lucca.

The city-gates were shut; but, on the word being given by her escort, they were thrown open, and she entered the dark and narrow streets of the town. "My prison!" thought Euthanasia. Here the company divided: Lauretta, at her own request, was conveyed to the house of the mother of Leodino; and Euthanasia was led to the palace prepared for her reception. She took no notice of the streets through which she passed, and cared little whether they conducted her to a palace or a prison; indeed during the latter part of her ride, her strength both of mind and body so much forsook her, that she could hardly keep her seat on her horse, but rode like a veiled statue of despair.

Euthanasia was led to her chamber; her attendants came to her, but she dismissed them all; and, her mind confused, her spirits and strength quite exhausted by long watching during several of the preceding nights, and by the exciting circumstances of the day, she threw herself dressed as she was on a couch, and, kindly nature coming to her aid, sank instantaneously into a heavy and dreamless sleep.

Day was far advanced, before she again awoke, and looked forth on the light, with a sentiment, as if the slight refreshment of spirit and strength she had received, were but a mockery of the sad weight that oppressed her heart. She lifted her heavy head, like a water lily whose cup is filled by a thunder shower: but, presently recalling her scattered faculties, she sat for some time in deep meditation, endeavouring to philosophize herself out of the unhappiness that she felt. The palace to which she had been conducted, was a large and magnificent one, near the outskirts of the town: it had belonged to one of the victims of Castruccio's despotism, and had the desolate and woe-begone appearance of a mansion which has lost its master. From the chamber where she sat, she looked upon the garden; a square plot of ground surrounded by four high walls, which had been planted in the Italian taste, but which now ran wild; the small flower-beds were overgrown with weeds, and the grass, a rude commoner, had thrust itself into the untrod paths; the stone-pedestals for the lemon-pots were green with moss and lichens; and here and there the wind-borne seed of some delicate plant had sown a lovely flower in the midst of the moist, coarse herbage which could ill claim its fellowship. A few cypress and box trees, which had been cut into shape, now mocked the gardener's knife with the unpruned growth of three years; and ivy darkened the walls side by side with the orange trees, whose golden apples shone amidst the dark foliage. A few lizards had crept from beneath the stones to bask in the rays of the autumnal sun; and the frogs croaked in a reservoir or cistern, which had once played as a fountain, but which was now choked with weeds and dirt. Such was the desolate scene which arrested the eyes of Euthanasia, as she looked from her window. "The image of my fortunes;" she thought, and turned away, while a tear flowed down her cheek.

Her servant now entered; and, while she arranged her dress, the woman related the catastrophe of the siege. When the soldiers of Castruccio had appeared behind her defenders coming down from the castle, they threw themselves first on those who guarded the bridge, and took Bondelmonti and the principal Florentines prisoners: but the dependents of the countess, transported with fury, and elevated by the promises which Bindo had held out of success, rushed out of their hiding-places, and charging those at the foot of the rock, drove them with desperate courage down the mountain path, unmindful of the enemies who pressed upon their rear. The battle was bloody; many fell on each side; the small troop of Valpergans were destroyed almost to a man, falling voluntary sacrifices for their mistress's preservation. A few were taken prisoners, and among them Bindo, who almost miraculously had escaped unwounded. But, if he were not wounded in body, his mind was almost frenzied with rage and disappointment, when he saw the Lucchese flag wave from the donjon of the castle; he tried to break from those who held him, and, weak as he appeared to be, he exerted such desperate strength, using both hands, feet, and teeth, that the soldiers found it necessary to bind him.—As they fastened the cords, Castiglione came up: he remembered the Albinois; and, asking why it was that he was used so roughly, he ordered them to set him free. As soon as his bonds were loosened, without speaking or looking round, he darted off; and, running across the country as swiftly as a deer from the hounds, was quickly out of sight.

Euthanasia wept when she heard of the blood that had been spilt for her; and self-reproach, who is ever ready to thrust in his sharp sting, if he find that mailed conscience has one weak part, now tormented her that she had not yielded, before one human life had been lost in so unhappy a cause. "Do not evil that good may come," thought she. "Are not those the words of the Teacher? I have done infinite evil, in spilling that blood whose each precious drop was of more worth than the jewels of a kingly crown; but my evil has borne its fitting fruit; its root in death, its produce poison."

In the course of the day, Arrigo Guinigi came to visit her. He came with a message from Castruccio, who intreated her to remain quietly in the palace provided for her, until he should return to Lucca, which would be in a few days, when he would learn from her own lips what her wishes were with regard to her future life. Arrigo said all this with downcast eyes and a heaving breast, hardly daring to speak, and much less raise his eyes upon the countess; who replied that she would obey; that she had much rather not see the prince; but that if he commanded it, she was ready to submit. "You see me, my dear Arrigo, a prisoner, despoiled of my possessions, a slave to your lord's will. Yet I hope and trust, that these events would not have created the deep sorrow with which I feel that my soul is filled, did not bitter sentiments of lost affections, disappointed expectations, and utter hopelessness, fill up the measure of my infelicity. My good youth, we are born to misery; so our priests tell us, and there is more sooth in that lesson, than in early youth we are willing to believe; yet fortitude is the virtue with which my father endeavoured principally to imbue me, and I would fain not disgrace his counsels; but indeed a poisoned barb has entered my heart, and I cannot draw it out."

Arrigo endeavoured to comfort her.—"Your state is far from hopeless; the prince has promised, and intends to keep his promise, that your revenues shall not be injured by the loss of your castle. At Florence you will be surrounded by friends, and every luxury and pleasure of life; and there you may again be happy."

Autumn was now far advanced, and the rains came on. The Florentine and Lucchese armies, which had remained looking at each other from opposite sides of the river, were now further divided by the overflowing of its waters; so each retreated to their several towns, and the campaign of that year ended. Castruccio returned to Lucca. His first concern was a long and private conversation with Castiglione; and immediately after he dispatched Arrigo to prepare Euthanasia for a conference.

Poor girl! her heart beat, and the blood mounted to her before pale cheeks, when she heard that she was to see him whom she had loved, and to whose memory, as of what had been, she clung with tenacious affection. It was a cruel task for her to behold his form, graceful as it had been when she gazed on it in happier days, and his countenance, which, but that more pride were mingled in the expression, was as gloriously beautiful, as when it beamed love upon her; and more than all, to hear his voice, whose soft and mellow cadences had wrapt her soul in Elysium, now to be heard as the voice of an alien. But indignation mingled itself with these feelings, and enabled her to support the coming trial with greater courage; so, calling up all of pride with which her delicacy might arm her, and all of fortitude which her philosophy had taught, she awaited with patience the expected moment.

She sat on a low sopha; her dress was dark; the vest, formed of purple silk, and fastened at her waist by a silken cord, fell in large folds to her feet; a cloak of sables hung on her shoulder; and her golden hair, partly clustered on her neck, and partly confined by a ribbon, covered with its ringlets her fair brow. When she heard the step of Castruccio approaching, she became pale; her very lips lost their colour; and her serious eyes, shorn of their beams, were as the deep azure of midnight, where the stars shine not. He entered. When he had seen her last, he had been haughty and imperious; but now his manner was all softness, gentleness and humility; so that, when he spoke, in spite of the high nobility of her spirit, her eyes were weighed down by the unshed tears.

"Countess," he said, "pardon me, if my intrusion upon you appear ungenerous; but persons, that, like myself, are occupied in the affairs of government, are apt to leave too much to underlings, who never do or say that which it were exactly right to have said or done. Your future peace is too dear to me, to permit me to hear from any but yourself what are your wishes and your expectations."

He paused, waiting for an answer, and fixed on her his soft and full eyes, which seemed to read her soul, while a gentle smile of compassion and love played on his lips. After collecting her thoughts, she raised her eyes to reply, and met those of her former lover, whose expression seemed fraught with all that affection he had once vowed to her. She was unable to speak; but then, angry at her own weakness, she rallied her spirits, and replied,—"I have but one favour to intreat, which is your permission to remove instantly to Florence."

"Your wishes in this respect, Madonna, are commands; yet I could have desired that you would consent to stay awhile in Lucca. I know the judgement that you have formed of me; you look on me as a wild beast ravenous for blood, as a lawless monster, despoiled of all the feelings of humanity. I could have desired that you would stay awhile, to find and to avow your injustice; I could wish you to stay, until the deep respect, and if you will permit the word, the love I feel for you, should make such impression on your heart, that you would allow me to assuage those sorrows of which I have unhappily been the cause."

"My lord, do not speak thus to me," replied Euthanasia, with a voice which at first trembled, but which gained firmness as she continued; "We are divided; there is an eternal barrier between us now, sealed by the blood of those miserable people who fell for me. I cannot, I do not love you; and, if a most frivolous and reprehensible weakness could make me listen now, the ghosts of the slain would arise to divide us. My lord, I cannot reason with you, I can hardly speak; the blood of the slaughtered, the tears of the survivors, the scathed ruins of my castle, are all answers, louder than words, to your present offers. If these have been your acts of courtship, pardon me if I say, that I had rather woo the lion in his den to be my husband, than become the bride of a conqueror. But this is useless cavilling, painful to both of us; it awakens in me the indignation I would fain repress; and it may kindle resentment in your heart, which is already too apt to be inflamed with that sentiment. You came, you say, to learn my wishes; you have now heard them; let us part; we part in that peace every Christian believer owes to his brother; I forgive you from my inmost heart; do not you hate me; and thus farewel."

"You forgive me, Euthanasia? Is then your soul so pure? me, who indeed have grievously wronged you; and, however necessary my actions have been, yet have they been destructive to you. But, if indeed you forgive me, and part in Christian amity, allow me once more to take your hand, that I may know that it is not a mere form of words, but that you express a feeling of the heart."

Euthanasia held out her hand, which he took in both his, and holding it thus, he said: "Hear me, my loved girl; you whom alone in the world I have ever loved. You despise, repulse, and almost hate me; and yet, God knows, I still cherish you as tenderly, as when we told each other's love-tale first in yonder unhappy castle. I do not ask you to love me, you cannot;—but you are still young, very young, Euthanasia; and fortune yet may have many changes in store for you. Remember, that, through them all, I am your friend; and if ever in any misery you want a protector, one to save and preserve you, Castruccio, the neglected, mistaken, but most faithful Castruccio, will ever be ready to use his arm and his power in your service. Now, Euthanasia, farewel."

"Oh God!" cried the unhappy girl, moved to her inmost heart, "could you not have spared me this? leave me; farewel for ever!"

He kissed her hand, and left her; while she, her delicate frame yielding under the many emotions she experienced, sank almost lifeless on the couch. She had suffered much, and borne up through all. But this last interview overcame her: her health, which had been weakened by watching, and agitation, and tears, now entirely gave way. A fever followed,—delirium, and utter deprivation of strength. The disease seemed to feed on her very vitals; and death already tainted her cheek with his fingers. But youth, and a constitution, nourished and strengthened among mountains, and healthful exertions of body and mind, saved her; and, after a confinement of several months, she again crept forth, to see the sun of spring smile on his children, who laughingly welcomed his genial beams.

Where during this time was the prophetess of Ferrara?

[10]See Dante.

END OF VOLUME II.

Milton Keynes UK
Ingram Content Group UK Ltd.
UKHW030742071024
449371UK00006B/636